SIMON FRASER UNIVERSITY
LIBRARY

IN HONOUR OF

VIRGINIA BRUSH ROSSI

Opportunity Cost
in Finance
and Accounting

OPPORTUNITY COST IN FINANCE AND ACCOUNTING

H.G. Heymann
AND
Robert Bloom

QUORUM BOOKS
New York • Westport, Connecticut • London

Library of Congress Cataloging-in-Publication Data

Heymann, H. G.
  Opportunity cost in finance and accounting / H.G. Heymann and
Robert Bloom
    p. cm.
  Includes bibliographical references and index.
  ISBN 0-89930-400-1 (lib. bdg. : alk. paper)
  1. Cost accounting. 2. Finance. 3. Opportunity costs.
I. Bloom, Robert. II. Title.
HF5686.C8H48   1990
658.15—dc20   90-36025

British Library Cataloguing in Publication Data is available.

Library of Congress Catalog Card Number: 90-36025
ISBN: 0-89930-400-1

First published in 1990

Quorum Books, 88 Post Road West, Westport, CT 06881
An imprint of Greenwood Publishing Group, Inc.

Printed in the United States of America

The paper used in this book complies with the
Permanent Paper Standard issued by the National
Information Standards Organization (Z39.48-1984).

10 9 8 7 6 5 4 3 2 1

Contents

Illustrations

TABLES

FIGURES

EXHIBITS

Preface

This book is about decision making, and business problem solving, emphasizing the concept of opportunity cost. While this subject is deeply rooted in economic theory, scientific methodology, philosophical beliefs, and generally accepted accounting principles (GAAP), this book attempts to present the material in an interesting and relevant manner.

At the outset, it should be recognized that the idea of opportunity cost is more than 200 years old. Defined as an integral part of classical economic theory that addresses problems resulting from scarcity, opportunity costs exist whenever the acceptance of one alternative precludes other alternatives. Thus, the concept of opportunity cost and its measurement are closely associated with the theory of choice, the concept of value, and the framework of rational decision making.

The main thrust of this book addresses the question of why a concept over 200 years old is not yet fully understood and why the opportunity cost concept is particularly relevant today. One of the reasons pertains to the development of increasingly sophisticated and affordable computer systems and their use in specialized business applications that are referred to as Decision Support Systems, Expert Systems, Knowledge-Based Information Systems, or Artificial Intelligence. Such computer applications do not solve specific problems, nor are they used to "explain" observed phenomena with the assistance of scientific methods. Instead, they are designed to aid specific individuals in their own particular and unique *problem-solving processes*. For example, instead of determining an optimal solution to a well-specified production problem using mathematical optimization methods such as linear programming, these specialized computer systems support individual decisionmakers in their own unique *judgmental processes* to explore complex and dynamically changing problem situations. Instead of solving problems or finding optimal solutions, these computer applications aid in the discovery of unique strategies to deal with poorly defined and ill-structured problem situations in terms of continuous improvements and specific management processes.

Within the framework of *practical problem solving,* opportunity cost becomes an important element that requires proper understanding. The practical use of opportunity cost goes far beyond theoretical arguments and equilibrium criteria that describe a balance between aggregate demand and aggregate supply within ideal competitive markets. While classical economic theory emphasizes the concept of an ideal free market economy, practical business problem solving must be concerned with the mangement of complex, interdependent, and dynamically changing problem situations that require approximate mangement processes as well as practical decision aids.

In contrast to developing *practical decision aids,* economic theory, following the lead of other scientific pursuits, utilizes generalized analytic models, structured theories, and simple arguments to explain the behavior of idealized economic agents (microeconomic models) or to predict the performance of more aggregated economic systems (macroeconomic models). It is the general complexity of human behavior, the unpredictability of the environment in which human organizations operate, as well as the lack of basic knowledge, that has resulted in a multitude of different models, theories, and concepts. By adopting specific beliefs and utilizing analogies with other fields of study, such as the use of mechanistic principles of Newtonian physics in economic theory, there has evolved a consistent set of arguments which are summarized in terms of the free market ideal. While this ideal has been integrated into a commonly accepted belief structure, practical limitations exist when this ideal is applied to practical problem solving. Only when problem situations are simple, well structured, and clearly defined is it possible to attain optimal solutions. Whenever problem situations become more complex, interdependent, poorly understood, and dynamically changing, the concern for optimality and specific problem solutions is replaced by concepts that address processes, strategies, and control procedures. This practical concern with managing introduces different interpretations of opportunity cost.

In order to clearly distinguish between theoretical ideals and practical needs a clear separation must be made between a *theoretical domain* and a *practical domain* of problem solving. While such separation has been made in technical areas by distinguishing, for example, between physics and engineering, in economics and finance such separation has not been made. As a consequence there exists the potential for misinterpreting existing theories including the concept of opportunity costs.

Inasmuch as economic theory is part of the ideal of individual freedom, rational behavior, and optimization models, so the concept of opportunity cost is integrated into the various topics of micro- and macroeconomics. The changing emphasis and the shifting problem environment faced by economic theories through time highlight the political and sociological nature that governs this subject. Since arguments in economics refer to common sense and intuitive examples, the difficulty with this subject lies in the rules that define a particular common sense. It is the wide variety of different philosophical positions, the availability of numerous models, and the use of different mathematical methods that makes the study of economics and human behavior so interesting and potentially confusing. Within this view, this book attempts to clarify issues associated with the opportunity cost principle, the measurement of opportunity costs, and its practical applications in the areas of finance and accounting.

This book is intended to make the concept of opportunity cost simple by providing sufficient examples to demonstrate specific issues. The insight this book seeks to convey involves concepts and terms not usually found in the related literature. This might limit the perceived usefulness of this book to those just interested in finding simple solutions to otherwise complex problems. On the other hand, the book addresses the concerns of a large number of individuals, professionals as well as students, who have recognized the limitations of conventional approaches that discuss rational decision making and opportunity cost measures in an idealized static equilibrium analysis. There is a discrepancy between models that attempt to explain normal, average, or marginal behavior in equilibrium and the practical needs of specific individuals faced with unique problem situations. The potential for misinterpreting existing theories and models becomes especially critical when practical problem-solving procedures are supported by advanced computer technology and large data banks, which utilize simple models originally developed to explain the virtures of the free market ideal.

To clarify the many issues that relate to the opportunity cost principle, this book starts with simple examples to introduce the framework in which opportunity cost has been defined. After basic concepts have been discussed, applications in economic theory, finance, and accounting are reviewed. As problem statements become increasingly more complex, multidimensional, and interdependent, the definition and measurement of opportunity cost become more difficult. In these circumstances, a more general understanding of the opportunity cost principle can help in the development of problem-solving strategies and practical management procedures. To clarify the many issues related to the opportunity cost principle, this book addresses:

1. The environment in which theories, models, and concepts are developed
2. The multiple dimensions of problem situations faced by practicing decisionmakers and managers
3. The various interpretations and applications of the opportunity cost principle in economic theory as well as formal finance and acounting models
4. The utilization of the opportunity cost principle in practical problem-solving processes and the formulation of strategic management procedures
5. The relevance of opportunity cost in computer-aided Decision Support Systems

Suitable as a supplementary text in advanced undergraduate and graduate courses in schools of business and public administration as well as in professional development seminars in financial decision making, accounting, and management, this book attempts to enhance the reader's appreciation of the many complex issues that relate to organizational management, financial decision making, valuation, and opportunity costs.

Our student assistants Kevin Brown and John R. Eslich at John Carroll University were helpful in conducting library research, preparing the bibliography, and proofreading the manuscript. We thank our principal wordprocessor, Ruth Cickavage, for doing her work meticulously.

PART I

Introduction to the Problem Environment

The subject of opportunity cost can be viewed as a part of the study of human behavior or as an element of economic theory related to decision making within an ideal market environment. While there are many aspects of human behavior, *economic decision making* originates from the belief that human wants and desires cannot be satisfied because of limited economic resources. It is scarcity that requires a choice among different alternatives. Whenever there is a pure choice situation, the acceptance of one alternative will exclude the acceptance of others. This, in turn, will result in opportunity costs, created by the perceived loss (cost) of not taking another alternative. Depending on the specifics of a choice situation, in economics it is scarcity that prevents the acceptance of other alternatives.

An economic choice problem resulting from scarcity can be viewed as having many dimensions that include technical, economic, organizational, social, and individual dimensions.

1. *Technical Dimensions*. Technical aspects result from the fact that things can be produced through different

manipulations of physical resources within the confines of physical and social laws. Technical or engineering-oriented problems are concerned with quantitative measures of resources as well as organizational and physical processes used to produce and distribute particular goods and services. While *technical concerns* relate to the economic and efficient production of competitive products, technical problems relate to such variables as production capacity, manufacturing processes, plant layout, material handling, and maintenance procedures as well as product design characteristics in terms of quality, safety, reliability, and general appeal. Practical business problem solving is largely related to finding solutions to technical problems using experimental techniques and quantitative methods.

2. *Economic Dimensions.* Economic aspects result from the existence of market-related phenomena. Resources and production outputs are traded in markets resulting in measures of value, income, and costs expressed in terms of money. Economic problems relate to resource availability, price behavior, and market competition, so that an economic analysis is concerned with the forecasting of future economic environments. *Economic variables* include market price behavior; market conduct, structure, and performance; as well as government regulations, restrictions, and subsidies; or market competition, growth, and dynamics. Economic variables are evaluated in terms of price levels, stability, and predictability as well as the potential for manipulating and changing the economic market environment through marketing and political strategies.

3. *Organizational Dimensions.* Organizational aspects result from the need to manage, coordinate, and control the many activities required to efficiently acquire, produce, and market economic goods and resources. Organizational concerns relate to the manageability of projects and the organizational design that affect production and transaction processes as well as management procedures, policies, and rules.

Organizational variables include the managerial functions of planning, organizing, staffing, directing, and controlling as well as the tasks of coordinating, motivating, communicating, and decision making. Organizational dimensions are evaluated in terms of organizational structures, subdivisions, specializations, authority relationships, management procedures, and, in general, the design of a management system. Such variables are analyzed with respect to management effectiveness, responsiveness, and flexibility or simply in terms of costs and benefits.

4. *Social Dimensions.* Social aspects result from the impact of specific choices made by the individual decisionmaker and society as a whole. *Social concerns* relate to such things as environmental protection, public health, education, occupational safety, and compliance with regulations, laws, codes, and ordinances. Social problems are usually evaluated in terms of costs and benefits that accrue to the general public over the service life of a particular project. Social dimensions assess contributions made to improving the quality of life within a society, resulting from the allocation, use, and distribution of available economic resources.

5. *Individual Dimensions.* Individual aspects result from the concern for individual rights as well as protections against discrimination, invasion of privacy, and the use of proprietary information. Such concerns affect choices and problem-solving procedures as well as policy decisions and employment practices

The multidimensionality of choice problems, which includes micro- and macroconcerns as well as international considerations, indicates the scope and variety of problem areas where opportunity cost principles can be applied. Much of the variety can be reduced by concentrating on the areas of finance and accounting and restricting the discussion to business-related decision making.

In accounting and finance, *choice problems* are usually stated in terms of costs and benefits expressed in money measures. This involves particular definitions of value and measures of costs and benefits as they accrue to economic entities. It is the concern with ownership rights and individual choices within a free market environment that has been the main emphasis in finance and accounting. By utilizing the structure of classical economic theory based on the work of Adam Smith (1723–1790), David Ricardo (1772–1823), Alfred Marshall (1842–1924), and Vilfredo Pareto (1848–1923), among others, the *free market ideal* is seen as a self-regulating mechanism for the efficient and optimal allocation of scarce economic resources based on individual preferences and freedom of choice. Over time, the arguments and interpretations of the free market ideal have changed from purely normative considerations to more scientific concerns. However, the normative values of the free market ideal are still strong, desirable, and beneficial and have been integrated into a commonly accepted belief structure.

By adopting the *analytic principle* as formulated by Aristotle (384–322 B.C.) and by utilizing the analytic-deductive approach to model building as popularized by Newton (1664–1727), individuals can reduce complex problem situations to simple and structured arguments. While this reductionist approach evolved over a long time period, it is the convincing simplicity of structured quantitative models that has made the analytic approach an accepted method also in social, economic, and political sciences. Strict rules exist on how to define a problem and how to solve it by using mathematical methods. As a consequence of using such structured quantitative models, we find that bounds exist on our ability to handle more complex, ill-structured, and dynamically changing problem situations.

This book distinguishes between the theoretical and the practical domain of problem solving. For example, the *theoretical domain of finance* is rooted in the arguments of classical economic theory, where the invisible hand of Adam Smith allocates scarce economic resources perfectly and optimally through the free market pricing mechanism. Given free, perfect, and complete competitive markets as well as individuals with complete rationality and perfect knowledge, besides a host of other necessary conditions, a closed economic system will reach an equilibrium and "Pareto optimality," if not in the short run at least in the long run. These required simplifications of reality must be seen as artificial simplifications introduced to attain specific argumentative and computational benefits. As part of a *normative theory,* such logical arguments are used to implement those necessary and sufficient conditions required to have economic systems functioning according to the free market ideal. In practice, this has led to the definition of ownership rights, antitrust laws, and a variety of government agencies such as the Securities and Exchange Commission and the Federal Trade Commission. Within the theoretical framework, individuals are viewed in terms of complete and perfect abilities and economic systems in terms of ideal competitive market structures.

In contrast, the *practical domain of finance* is confronted with dynamic, complex, ill-structured, and poorly understood problem situations. This more realistic view of decision problems does not fit conveniently into the structure of theoretical models. Even if certain economic entities have benefited in the past from specific analytic models, functional specializations, formal organizational hierarchies, and structured management procedures, it is the complex interrelatedness within economic systems, especially in times of rapid and unpredictable change, that requires decisionmakers to confront those ill-structured, poorly defined, and complex decision situations. Practitioners as *pragmatists* have been using structured mathematical models either because of the lack of better alternatives or because they realize the value of these models in subjective, judgmental, or political decision processes. Since there are no clear rules prescribing the level of abstractions or the extent of simplifications required to state a problem, to solve a problem, or to recognize a problem, a theory of practical problem solving must recognize the reality of technical and environmental changes over time. This is of special interest to a decisionmaker who utilizes modern computer technology in conjunction with traditional analytic and conceptual models.

It is the strict application of analytic simplifications that have led to partial equilibrium models, micro- and macroanalysis as well as a multitude of explanations that address economic problems in the present, the short run, or the long run. Depending on the specific model characteristics stated in terms of different *mathematical methods,* such as functional analysis, set theory, statistics, or probability theory among others, models address states, stocks, and flows; individuals, groups, and organizations; as well as processes, mechanisms, and relationships. All these different approaches bring along their own definitions and their own arguments. Lacking the ability to rationally or objectively select from among conflicting theories with the help of experimentation such as used in physical sciences, we find that the conflict between different theories and concepts in social sciences is left to political, economic, and social aspects, as well as to historical experience.

Within this general view of a complex and dynamically changing world of practical and theoretical concerns, the next two chapters present an introduction to the opportunity cost principle within the framework of rational choice and a review of the opportunity cost principle as applied in classical economic theory.

1

Opportunity Cost and the Theory of Rational Choice

The essence of the opportunity cost principle implies that the value or cost of a resource used in one particular application is determined by its use in the best alternative given up. The basis for understanding this concept lies in the recognition that every act of choice also involves an act of sacrifice.

It seems clear that any individual can do only particular things during a specific time period. For instance, watching a football game excludes other activities, such as working in the office. Using the opportunity cost principle, the individual figures that the cost of watching the game is not only the explicit price of the ticket but also the earnings given up by not working. However, one cannot work all the time, and recreation is important, as is the potential for goodwill created by taking someone else to the game. Thus, the opportunity cost principle involves economic and noneconomic considerations.

The *theory of rational choice* implies that any individual who has free choice will always select the alternative that provides the largest benefits, that is, utility or value. Thus, if we observe an individual going to a football game, this choice must be preferred to all others, including working. Take the example in which a ticket to the game is $10, and working could earn $30. Then the actual cost of going to the game is not $10, but $40, considering also the lost earnings as opportunity cost. We can write this problem in terms of two choice alternatives:

1. Work and earn $30
2. Go to the game, spend $10, and receive psychic benefits (U)

(U) represents the nonmonetary benefits gained from going to the game. Knowing that the game was preferred, we can state that the *psychic benefits* must have been larger than $40 or $U \geq \$40$. At the margin or at the limit, $U = \$40$. At this point the individual would be indifferent between the two choice alternatives. Thus, if we observe particular choices made, it is possible to make statements about an individual's preferences, that is, revealed preference.

Neglecting a number of technical assumptions and special definitions, the theory of rational choice is concerned with *preferences* that determine the final selection from among choice alternatives. As long as a "rational" individual prefers more to less (utility, value, money), we can make predictions with respect to choices that will be made. For example, consider the following observations:

1. High-income professionals are more likely to hire someone to type letters, cut grass, and paint their houses than are low-income people
2. Low-income individuals tend to travel long distances by bus or train, while high-income professionals are more likely to travel by airplane

An explanation for these observations can be stated in terms of opportunity costs. It is expensive for highly paid professionals to spend time on a bus, to type letters, or to paint houses. Consider that one hour spend on mowing a lawn could involve a sacrifice of a $300 fee for a highly paid professional, while a lawn service may only charge $20 for the same hour. Thus, the relevant cost for selecting an optimal choice alternative is not only the cash expenditure but also the opportunity cost involved by foregoing something else. By ignoring nonmonetary (psychic) costs and benefits that may be associated with certain activities, it is possible to concentrate only on *monetary measures*. This is usually done since psychic values are difficult to measure and to express in equivalent money terms. While it may be difficult to predict consistently individual behavior and preferences, quite accurate predictions can be made for the average behavior of a large group of people as long as psychic costs and benefits are randomly distributed.

To make predictions of choices, it is necessary to include a measure of opportunity costs. For example, the relevant comparison of alternative transportation costs is not busfare, $100; airfare $200; but airfare $200 and busfare $100 as well as the opportunity cost of taking the bus instead of the plane. Assuming the bus ride takes one hour longer, a highly paid professional may forego a fee of $300. For this individual the busfare is $100 + $300 = $400 compared to the airfare of $200. Since the opportunity cost for low-income individuals is comparatively lower, the observed behavior of both low- and high-income individuals can be explained by the theory of rational choice. While there are other possible explanations and individual exceptions, such as getting sick on airplanes, the argument based on rational behavior and monetary values has been accepted as a valid explanation for many observed phenomena at least on the average.

By extending this argument to costs and benefits based on subjective measures, the postulate of rational behavior can be made a universal tautology: "Rational individuals *always* select the optimal alternative." It is the opportunity cost principle that recognizes the fact that the use of scarce resources, including time, cannot be evaluated in isolation. The explicit cost or cash outlay associated with the use of an economic resource is an inadequate measure of the actual costs involved

In general, the opportunity cost principle stems from the fact that the use of an economic resource in one application precludes its use within another. For example, on a macrolevel, a society's decision to increase its production of food may reduce its production of clothing. In this case, the cost of producing an increased amount of food can be expressed in terms of the effects resulting from the decreased production of clothing. For a society to be "better off" after the switch, the decrease in the price of food should be larger than the increase in the price of clothing. Thus, it is the joint effect resulting from an interrelationship between alternative uses of economic resources that leads to alternative costs or opportunity costs. Similar arguments have been made in terms of guns versus butter.

In the literature, we find the following definition of opportunity costs or alternative costs: "The alternative cost [opportunity cost] of using resources in a certain way is the value of what these resources could have produced if they had been used in the best alternative" (Mansfield, 1977, p. 11).

On a microlevel, decision alternatives relate to individual economic agents such as firms or individuals. Their individual actions will not affect price levels, so that decision alternatives relate to different uses of resources when market prices are fixed. For example, in the literature we can find the following definition: "The opportunity cost of using any input in a particular production process is the output foregone from not using the input in some alternative production process (since it cannot be used in two production processes simultaneously)" (Maurice and Smithson, 1981, p. 227).

Generally, opportunity costs can be defined as "those benefits which could have been received had an alternative course of action been chosen" (Thompson, 1973, p. 263). Considering that there are potentially many different alternative uses for a scarce economic resource, the opportunity cost is determined by the most valuable benefits sacrificed, so that:

> the [opportunity] cost of committing resources to any particular use is determined by the value of the resources in their best alternative use. By committing them to one use, all other possible uses

> are excluded. Some of these excluded uses are more valuable than others. It is the most valuable of them which is alone relevant in determining what has been sacrificed by committing the resources elsewhere—or in determining the "cost" of committing them elsewhere. (Solomons, 1966)

Thus, the relevant opportunity cost can only be determined by considering the specific details of a specific problem situation. This individuality of problem definitions contributes to the complications associated with the measurement of relevant opportunity costs.

The postulate that individuals are acting rationally and are always selecting the optimal alternative can only be maintained when including an opportunity cost measure in the comparison of choice alternatives. However, as long as opportunity costs are a matter of different individuals' preferences, based on subjective measures and including psychic concerns, it is difficult to verify such a proposition. As it stands, the proposition of rational behavior is an accepted tautology: "Rational individuals will always select the optional choice alternative." *Tautologies* are statements that are true by definition, but which cannot be verified. They are accepted as a matter of beliefs. The practical usefulness of such tautologies must be reconciled with the experience of individuals. In economic models, the postulate of rational behavior is beneficial because it allows the development of theories that clearly define optimal solutions. By combining the theory of rational choice with concepts of ideal competitive markets, it is possible to derive optimal market equilibrium models.

THE THEORY OF RATIONAL CHOICE

The theory of rational choice follows a long history of analytic model building and attempts to explain (predict) observed behavior of individuals. Discussions and mathematical treatments can be traced to the eighteenth century and to such individuals as Daniel Bernoulli (1700–1782) and Jeremy Bentham (1748–1832). While expressed in various and different forms using different mathematical methods, rational choice problems can be stated in the mathematical *set theory* in terms of a choice set that contains all relevant and feasible choice alternatives as well as axioms of preference ranking. Following strict mathematical rules associated with the *theory of ranking numbers*, specific characteristics of the choice set and the axioms of preference can be established.

Choice Sets. Each alternative in a choice set must be independent and fully defined, so that it can be expressed in terms of numbers (scalars or vectors). All alternatives are therefore stated in numbers (values) and ranked according to the number system. Thus, following the rules of ranking numbers, the characteristics of a choice set can be associated with the following attributes: (1) complete: all alternatives are fully defined; (2) perfect: all alternatives are attainable without further cost; (3) free: all alternatives are assessable without barriers.

Axioms of Preference Ranking. Alternatives within the choice set have assigned values (numbers) that are ranked according to a preference ordering system, which corresponds to the hierarchical order of numbers. While there are different ways to express preferences and measures of value, interpretations of the axioms of preference ranking usually refer to the following principles defining rational behavior:

1. *Ability Principle:* a rational decisionmaker is able to compare and rank all alternatives without effort (comparability)

2. *Consistency Principle:* a rational decisionmaker is able to rank alternatives consistently (transitivity)

3. *Dominance Principle:* a rational decisionmaker always prefers more to less (nonsatiation of wants)

4. *Indifference Principle:* a rational decisionmaker is able to trade off attributes of alternatives to attain levels of indifference (indifference curves)

5. *Diminishing Marginal Preferences:* a rational decisionmaker prefers more, but at a decreasing strength of preference (concave indifference curves)

While specifications of the choice set and the preference structure stem from the requirements of mathematical procedures and the theory of numbers, there are necessary implications pertaining to the *behavioral characteristics* and abilities of rational decisionmakers, who are goal-oriented, optimizing, have ideal cognitive abilities, and evaluate all alternatives in isolation.

Economic models concerned with the efficient and optimal allocation of scarce economic resources through free market forces use the logical structure of the theory of rational choice to determine the necessary and sufficient conditions that must prevail in order to attain the desired solution. Given that rational individuals always want more and that they compete in perfect markets for scarce resources and goods, they establish an equilibrium price level that is determined through aggregate demand and supply conditions. Recognizing the timeless and spaceless framework of this mathematical concept, the necessary and sufficient characteristics of an ideal market can be described by the following characteristics:

1. *Complete Markets:* the market opportunity set is completely defined, and all alternatives are perfectly divisible and independent

2. *Perfect Markets:* the market opportunities are attainable without additional costs (no taxes, no transaction costs), defining the concept of frictionless markets

3. *Free Markets:* the market opportunity set is assessible without barriers, and any amount of money can be borrowed or lent, restricted only by resource ownership

4. *Competitive Markets:* all market participants are small atomistic price-takers, rational and fully informed

5. *Market Equilibrium:* a state where prices of all goods are fixed and determined by aggregate demand equal to aggregate supply

The analysis of economic systems in terms of static equilibrium states follows a long history of thought that is also reflected in basic principles of mechanical physics as introduced by Newton (1642–1727). Based on the belief in analytic methods and atomistic elements of nature that are strictly related through mechanical, deterministic, and causal relationships, an economic system is seen to evolve to an equilibrium state, at least in the long run, if left to free market forces. Given the necessary and sufficient assumptions about rational economic behavior and free, complete, and perfectly competitive markets, it is possible to describe specific characteristics of a long-run equilibrium state. While a variety of approaches exists, a classical long-run market equilibrium can be expressed in terms of average market participants (consensus pricing) or in terms of marginal market participants (exchange pricing). The difference lies within the assumptions with respect to individual dissimilarities. The analysis of a free, perfect, and complete competitive market environment provides the necessary and sufficient conditions to attain a *Pareto optimal* allocation of scarce economic resources. In a Pareto optimal allocation, at least one individual is better off through free trade and nobody is worse off, given a particular resource ownership distribution. Seen as a social welfare optimum, the practical usefulness of such arguments to an individual decisionmaker is limited. A Pareto optimal allocation of resources occurs freely through trade by completely informed individuals pursuing their own selfish interests.

Having defined the *mathematical requirements* of an ideal competitive market equilibrium, we recognize that there are *necessary implications* that follow for the behavior of individual economic agents (microeconomic analysis) and for the characteristics of a market equilibrium (macroeconomic analysis).

On an individual level

1. Rational market participants react passively to given market prices
2. Rational market participants utilize resources in the most efficient way to optimize their own benefits
3. Rational market participants earn normal competitive returns on all resources owned

On a market level

1. In equilibrium all perfect substitutes sell at the same price (Law of One Price)

2. In equilibrium all resources are optimally allocated so that no market opportunity costs exist; this assumes that all economic agents are equally concerned only with market prices and economic profits (consensus pricing)
3. In equilibrium all resources are optimally priced, reflecting all relevant information (informational efficiency of markets)
4. In equilibrium all traded resources earn the normal competitive market return, and excess economic profits are equal to zero

The conditions of equilibrium and optimality as determined in ideal competitive markets can be stated in various ways depending on the mathematical methods used. Traditional economic analysis applies *functional analysis* which describes the characteristics of production, cost, and revenue functions. In equilibrium the marginal contribution of different sources to profit must be equal and zero.

$$\left[\; \frac{\partial f}{\partial x} \; = 0 \text{ is a mathematical condition of optimality} \right]$$

The requirements of differentiability in functional analysis have been eliminated by adopting mathematical *set theory* (Von Neumann and Morgenstern, 1953). This allows the treatment of problems involving more of the multidimensionality of real business problems, but requires also a broader definition of costs and benefits, as well as the abilities of rational decisionmakers to evaluate and rank more complex alternatives. Thus, changing the mathematical structure in which choice problems are defined requires a reassessment of the role markets play, which implies concepts that go far beyond the ideals treated by classical economic theory.

DEFINITIONS OF COSTS AND BENEFITS IN ACCOUNTING

In economic theory, by utilizing the framework of rational behavior and ideal competitive markets in equilibrium, the costs and benefits of economic activities are clearly defined by market prices. In accounting, the concepts of costs and benefits differ from those concepts in economic theory, recognizing that early accounting practices evolved from concepts of bookkeeping and a stewardship role of accountants to business owners. Accounting has changed over time by recognizing the effects of accounting information on management procedures, on security pricing decisions, or on social accountability and welfare. Thus, interpretations, measures and definitions of costs and benefits presented in accounting reports have changed. When addressing the cost of producing goods and services in accounting, it is usual to distinguish between the following definitions.

Explicit Costs. These costs are recognized by accountants as expenses, since they are based on actual transactions to acquire resources used in the production process. For example, a firm's payroll, payments for raw and semifinished materials, and payments for services acquired such as overhead and depreciation allowances make up a firm's production expenses that are separated in accounting statements.

Implicit Costs. These are costs that are incurred because of particular policies and procedures used. They are not directly measurable in terms of cash outlays or transactions and are therefore not recorded by accountants. For example, the loss of goodwill, the loss of potential customers, or the loss of motivation by employees can be considered implicit costs. These costs affect the profitability of a business through reduced revenues or increased explicit costs because of reduced productivity and increased waste. These costs represent a *type of opportunity cost,* since resources are not used optimally. Implicit costs occur when resources are not used efficiently or effectively to reach the goal of optimal profits. The impact of these costs on business performance is difficult to assess, without reference to some outside standards. It is the role of cost accounting and management control procedures to assess and reduce the impact of these implicit costs.

Opportunity Costs. These are costs of self-owned resources that are not acquired in markets and that accountants do not report. For example, accounting reports are concerned with the return of accounting profits to owners. Therefore, the salary of a proprietor or the return to invested capital are not part of a firm's explicit production costs. However, the costs of self-owned resources are real costs of production, since these resources are not free. The definition of economic profits recognizes these costs. When a resource is used in the production of a particular product, it cannot be used at the same time in other alternatives. Therefore, the value of a self-employed resource can be assessed by the value foregone of not using the resource in its best alternative use. This form of valuation is addressed by the *opportunity cost principle* and is related to the Law of One Price.

The recognition and reporting of specific costs and benefits in accounting is determined by generally accepted accounting principles (GAAP), which have evolved over time and which are specified by the accounting profession, the Accounting Principles Board (APB), or the Financial Accounting Standards Board (FASB), with suggestions from the Securities and Exchange Commission (SEC) and other authoritative bodies. Thus, accounting procedures are largely founded on an *authoritarian approach* and are not theory-based. Therefore, reported financial accounting data are limited to explicit costs based on historical transactions, while financial decision making must recognize the impact of all costs, including opportunity costs. Thus, accounting numbers must be adjusted, depending on the particular decision to be made or the particular business problem to be solved.

Consider, for example, the following situation in which an investor is contemplating the purchase of a small firm, which is currently operated as a proprietorship by an owner-manager. In reviewing the financial accounting information, the investor considers the following points to be important:

1. Explicit Production Costs. While the reported production costs reflect accounting principles, the investor believes that the currently used

production method can be changed and made more efficient, thereby reducing actual production costs.

2. Implicit Production Costs. Because of an obvious lack of motivation by employees, inefficiencies and outright waste exist. The investor believes that those costs can be eliminated by improving management procedures.

3. Opportunity Costs. Because the current owner's expenses for his work are not included directly in the accounting data, the investor determines that the skills of the current owner-manager can be acquired in the market by paying a competitive salary to a professional manager.

After making the necessary adjustments to the reported cost figures, the investor believes that the revenues can be increased by a more aggressive marketing effort. As a result of this analysis, the investor concludes that he can earn an adequate return on his investment. He, therefore, offers the current owner a sum of money which reflects the investor's *opportunity cost of money,* as well as the timing and risk associated with projected future income streams. While this example does not use any numbers, it highlights some of the arguments the investor should or will employ when evaluating the purchase of the firm. The measurement of explicit costs is discussed in accounting principles, the tax code, and economic theory, which involve different objectives and different frames of reference. We are concerned only with the measurement of opportunity costs and in particular the opportunity cost of money.

COMPETITIVE MARKET EQUILIBRIUM AND OPPORTUNITY COST

Simple examples are concerned with explicit costs and benefits that are associated with a specific activity at a specific point in time. Usually such examples are treated within the framework of ideal competitive markets and in terms of equilibrium market prices. By assuming equilibrium and rational behavior, these simple examples involve a buyer and a seller who exchange economic resources or goods at the prevailing market price. Thus, the costs to the buyer are equal to the benefits of the seller. The buyer evaluates the transaction with respect to all other available alternatives, thus considering, in addition to the explicit costs, the opportunity costs of doing something else with the money or the time. These simple examples are rather specific in defining a particular problem situation.

Given the large number of possible simple problem statements, it is the specification of the environment in which a problem is stated which defines costs, benefits, and opportunity costs. By being concerned only with equilibrium market prices determined by aggregate supply equal to aggregate demand within ideal competitive markets, we can make several postulates:

1. All market participants face the same equilibrium prices which are fixed

2. All market participants are only concerned with market prices to determine explicit costs and market-related opportunity costs

3. All market participants are rational, concerned only with money and the optimization of benefits that can be obtained from money

4. All market participants are "equal" in terms of the goals, but possess different amounts of economic resources they control with ownership rights

The solution to a particular problem is, therefore, dependent on the specific assumptions that specify the problem. Given the ideal environment of perfect competitive markets in equilibrium and rational individuals possessing a single goal and full information, it is possible to determine an optimal solution, using the Law of One Price or the idea that in equilibrium no opportunity costs exist.

The *Law of One Price* provides a basis for assessing opportunity costs of economic goods that are not directly traded or are traded only very infrequently, such as in self-employment. For example, the value of the work of a self-employed proprietor can be assessed by a comparison with the salary that could be earned in the market or by the salary that must be paid to a professional manager doing the same type of work. A similar application is the valuation of real estate that is not traded. By finding *perfect substitutes* in the vicinity, a comparison can be made and a fair market price established. The Law of One Price has many other applications for assessing comparative market prices such as determining the fair rent of housing, the value of a new security offering, or the price of antiques that are not regularly traded.

When choice problems involve a certain length of time in which economic resources (money) are invested (*single time period models*), a difference in market prices can be established, leading to potential gains or losses. Such price differences can be expressed in terms of money ($) or in terms of percentage returns (%), representing absolute and relative numbers. Under the assumption that all prices are known, not only today but also in the future (assumption of certainty and full knowledge), such gains and losses can be stated as:

$$\text{gain/loss} = P_1 - P_0 \ [\$] \qquad \text{(absolute numbers)}$$

$$\text{gain/loss} = \frac{P_1 - P_0}{P_0} \ [\%] \qquad \text{(relative numbers)}$$

where P_0 is the price today and P_1 the price at the end of the period. The introduction of prices in the future and the varying length of time periods, together with the potential to earn income during the time period, create a large number of new problem statements and new measures of gains and losses, as well as problems that address uncertainty, reinvestment, forecasting, diversification, forward markets, and option markets, among many other possibilities. It is the wide variety of potential problem statements and different problem environments that individual decisionmakers may face, which has made the field of financial decision making and problem solving such an interesting subject to study.

THE OPPORTUNITY COST OF MONEY

In terms of a simple example to demonstrate a measure of the opportunity cost of money, consider the following case. An individual is faced with the following choice problem:

A] Buy a commodity today at a price P_0, store the commodity, and sell it at a price P_1 at the end of the period. The cost of storing the commodity is C [$].

B] Invest the equivalent amount of money in the financial market and earn an interest payment of I [$].

Given that all numbers are known with certainty, the alternative B represents a measure of the opportunity cost of money. Since money can always be invested in the market by lending it to someone else, the financial market represents a logical reference point to make comparisons among investment alternatives. Thus it is the opportunity to earn interest in the financial market that represents a measure of the opportunity cost of money. Only an irrational individual will keep money at home under the mattress and thus forego the interest payment.

A comparison of the two alternatives reveals which of the two is more profitable:

A] gain $= P_1 - C - P_0$ [$]
B] gain $= P_0 + I - P_0$ [$]

The difference between the two alternatives represents a measure of opportunity cost [OPC], if the more profitable alternative is not taken, or:

$$OPC = A] - B] = P_1 - C - I - P_0$$

Given the assumption of ideal markets in equilibrium and the fact that under certainty the two alternatives must be perfect substitutes, the opportunity cost must be equal to zero so that:

$$P_0 = P_1 - C - I$$

or

$$P_1 = P_0 + C + I$$

This follows logically from the assumptions and can be summarized by the Law of One Price or the statement that in equilibrium the opportunity cost between perfect substitutes must be equal to zero. While this statement must hold in equilibrium and in a world of certainty, many conditions exist that potentially lead to different situations when considering a more complex reality.

Arguments exist which show that *equilibrium* must exist, given the postulates of ideal competitive markets. For example, if by chance

$$P_1 > P_0 + C + I$$

then alternative A] is preferred. Given that all investors would recognize this fact and would try to exploit this excess profit opportunity, prices would adjust to reach the equilibrium; similarly, but in reverse, when alternative B] is preferred. Thus the profit motive and market forces will assure that alternative investment opportunities (perfect substitutes) must be traded at equal prices, given the assumptions of perfect markets and rational individuals.

The interpretation of this simple example leads to different explanations that can occur with respect to the processes (mechanisms) by which the market reaches an equilibrium. Since there are four variables which all can adjust in response to changes in the aggregate market supply and demand conditions, the commodity prices P_0, P_1, the cost of storage C, and the interest I may adjust. Furthermore, while the example may hold for an ideal economic system in the aggregate, it may not hold for individuals. Thus while conclusions of the argument follow logically from the assumptions on which the argument is based, there remain very basic questions, such as:

1. Does the real world which is dynamically changing, complex, and uncertain work this way?
2. Do all prices actually adjust efficiently and timely as suggested by the model?
3. When does such an ideal equilibrium really exist?

Answers to these questions are difficult, if not impossible. It is therefore a matter of belief in the *normative values* associated with the free market ideal that leads to the acceptance of specific arguments. As a normative theory, the ideal of the free markets and the argument of equilibrium, at least in the long run, provides a logical basis that guides the creation of institutions, regulations, and the definition of the role of government.

THE VALUE OF MONEY

Besides the implications of simple equilibrium arguments on decision making, there is the possibility for expressing different measures of the opportunity cost of money. Given a simple one-period model under certainty, the opportunity cost of money can be stated in terms of two alternatives:

A]   Do nothing, keep the money at home under a mattress

B]   Invest the money in the market, and earn interest income I [$]

The opportunity cost is the difference between the two alternatives or I [$]. Given that interest payments are contractually fixed for the period and stated in terms of a *nominal interest rate* i [%] we can define:

$$I = i.P_0 \ [\$]$$

or

$$i = \frac{I}{P_0} \ [\%]$$

In this case, I [$] represents the payment in money at the end of the period for lending (or borrowing) the money. The money position at the end of the period can be viewed as the *terminal wealth* $W_1 = P_0 (1 + i)$, starting with an initial wealth $W_0 = P_0$, so that:

$$W_1 = W_0 + I = W_0 (1 + i)$$

The nominal interest rate (i) is stated in terms of percent (%) and represents the *nominal opportunity cost of money.*

There is, however, the question of what determines the value of money. This again can be answered in terms of the opportunity cost principle. One particular theory refers to the consumption possibility of money value. Consider the following example: A rational individual is faced with the following two alternatives:

A] Spend the money W_0 today on current consumption and get psychic benefits today, or

B] Invest the money W_0 in the market, earn interest income I [$] to attain W_1, which can be consumed at time t_1

By foregoing current consumption, the individual may increase consumption at time t_1. The amount of consumption depends, however, on the current price level P_0 and the future price level P_1 so that:

$$W_0 = C_0 \cdot P_0 \qquad W_1 = C_1 \cdot P_1$$

or

$$C_0 = \frac{W_0}{P_0} \qquad C_1 = \frac{W_1}{P_1}$$

In order to save money or to transfer current consumption (C_0) to consumption tomorrow (C_1), there must be a *real gain* (r [%]); otherwise there would be no incentive to save, given rational individuals, full knowledge of future prices, and certainty. With the following definitions:

$$C_1 = C_0 (1 + r)$$
$$P_1 = P_0 (1 + dp)$$
$$W_1 = W_0 (1 + i)$$

where
r = real "rate of return" [%]

dp = price changes (inflation rate) [%]

i = nominal interest [%]

we can derive that in equilibrium:

$$i = r + dp$$
or
$$r = i - dp$$

Thus, the *real opportunity cost of money* is equal to the nominal interest rate (i) minus the inflation rate (dp). As one can readily see, the question of measuring the opportunity cost becomes more complicated as more of the idealizing assumptions are relaxed. Within the consumption theory of money value, the opportunity cost of money depends on the level of nominal interest and expected inflation rates.

SUMMARY

In general, the opportunity cost principle compares different choice alternatives within the framework of rational choice. Depending on the specific problem statement and assumptions that specify a particular problem, various measures of opportunity cost can be defined. Within the concept of a market equilibrium, any individual would be just indifferent between different choice alternatives presented by the market. This implies that all individuals have preference structures defined in terms of money value and prefer more money to less. By applying this argument to the aggregate market environment, we can postulate that in equilibrium all market opportunity costs are just equal to zero. Thus, given equilibrium market prices, all individual decisionmakers can take market prices and use them to evaluate different choice alternatives (microeconomic analysis). If individuals see that certain choices are preferred (more profitable), then it can be argued that all market participants would want to exploit this profitable alternative, so that prices adjust (macroeconomic analysis). In equilibrium, all prices have adjusted so that the Law of One Price holds and no market opportunity costs exist.

The potentially *circular reasoning* is recognized by admitting that micro- and macroeconomic analysis are two separate fields of study. Only in equilibrium does everything fall together, so that equilibrium is a preferred analysis. In equilibrium all prices have properly adjusted. Economic decisions to be made consider individuals, who are not yet in equilibrium with respect to the market. By assuming that individual economic agents are small (atomistic) with respect to the market, individuals adjust passively to given market prices by eliminating their own opportunity costs in terms of optimizing their own financial positions. Thus, while *equilibrium analysis* provides the basis for many arguments that reflect the normative values of the free market ideal, it is *disequilibrium* and the need to make economic decisions that is of concern to individual decisionmakers and to practical problem solving.

2

Opportunity Cost and Economic Theory

The concept of opportunity cost has been discussed by David Ricardo (1772–1823) and other economists in the early 1800s in order to explain the benefits of trade between nations having different levels of productivity. Ricardo dealt with trade between England and Portugal. He considered an example where England exports wool and Portugal exports port wine, and where each country has only one factor of production, that is, labor. Between the two countries a difference exists in labor productivity, as shown in Table 2.1.

Table 2.1
Wool and Wine Production in England and Portugal

	One English Worker Produces	One Portuguese Worker Produces
Wool	6 bales	1 bale
Wine	3 casks	1 cask

An English worker can produce either six bales of wool or three casks of wine. Thus, the opportunity cost of producing one more cask of wine is equal to giving up two bales of wool. Since six bales are equal to three casks, the opportunity cost of producing one cask of wine is equal to two bales of wool. In Portugal, one worker can produce either one bale of wool or one cask of wine. Thus, the opportunity cost for producing one more cask of wine is equal to the sacrifice of one bale of wool. The opportunity cost in each country is shown in Table 2.2.

From this opportunity cost table, a sharp entrepreneur can readily see opportunities for trade. The entrepreneur would buy a cask of wine in Portugal for one bale of wool; the wine then could be sold for two bales of wool in England, and so on. Ricardo assumed that the differences in prices between the two countries are based on differences in the productivity of labor. He used this argument to explain the motives and benefits of international trade.

Even though a worker in England is more productive than a worker in Portugal, trade provides benefits to both countries. In absolute terms, the English worker is more productive than the Portuguese worker in both the wine and wool production. However, in relative terms, an English worker is six times more productive in wool and three times more productive in wine than the Portuguese worker. Thus, if we compare industries, the English worker is relatively more productive in the wool industry than in the wine industry. Therefore, England has a *comparative advantage*

Table 2.2
Opportunity Cost of Production in England and Portugal

England	1 bale of wool costs 1/2 cask of wine
	1 cask of wine costs 2 bales of wool
Portugal	1 bale of wool costs 1 cask of wine
	1 cask of wine costs 1 bale of wool

in wool production and Portugal a comparative advantage in wine production. Stated differently, even though Portugal is less productive in both industries (an absolute comparison), it has a comparative advantage or less of a disadvantage in producing wine (a relative comparison). By shifting labor and producing more wine, Portugal can trade for wool with England. In similar fashion, England finds it beneficial to concentrate on its wool production and trade wool for wine. As a result, both countries are better off.

OPPORTUNITY COST AND THE PRINCIPLE OF COMPARATIVE ADVANTAGE

The principle of comparative advantage applies the concept of *relative opportunity costs*. Consider an example where individuals freely trade instead of countries. Free individuals trade only if they are better off through trade, or else they would not do it (the postulate of rational behavior). Take the case of a prominent physician who is also an exceptionally good typist. Since more money can be earned in the medical profession than in typing, it is beneficial to concentrate on doctoring and hiring a secretary to type. The secretary has a job, and the doctor can readily afford to pay the salary of the secretary out of the fees earned. Thus, both are better off. The professional has a comparative advantage in practicing the higher-paid work. In relative terms, the opportunity cost of professional work is higher than other work, ignoring any psychic benefits or costs.

While the examples establish the fact that trade is beneficial, the question remains: *who benefits more from trade?* While trade between individuals should distribute the gain by an arm's-length negotiation, trade between nations involves a different type of a problem. While mathematically a nation can be viewed as one individual economic unit that makes rational decisions, nations do represent diverse groups of individuals, industries, and governments. Thus, while a nation as a whole may be better off through international trade, there are usually some individuals who are worse off. Those who are hurt by international competition naturally do not like it. They will seek protection through government regulations. It is, therefore, important to clarify terms used by economists when they argue that a country is better off with free trade. Take the case in which losers are compensated by the winners for their losses. If all losers become at least as well off as before the trade and at least one of the gainers is better off, then society as a whole is clearly better off. This concept relates to the principle of *Pareto optimality.* A society is better off if no member is worse off and some are better off after the implementation of a particular economic policy. Thus, the original distribution of wealth is not changed, except some members are better off. In may cases, the required compensation of losers by gainers is not carried out, so that it is not surprising that losers oppose free trade. As a consequence, the conditions of trade and the distribution of benefits to be gained by society become part of the political process.

In the example of trading wool and wine between England and Portugal, it becomes obvious that some workers in the wine industry will have to find new employment. In realistic terms, this may involve moving, learning a new trade, or being at least temporarily unemployed. A small, one-industry town may even be devastated because of import competition. On the other hand, factors of production in the exporting industry are better off because of expanded employment. Furthermore, lower prices for imported goods benefit the users of such goods. Given that markets are competitive, lower resource prices will be reflected in lower consumer prices. Thus, consumers as a group will always be better off as a result of international trade.

While the *principle of comparative advantage* has been cast into a model of international trade between two countries and labor as the only factor of production, similar conclusions can be derived as soon as the problem is stated in terms of the opportunity cost principle. Once opportunity costs are defined as reflecting the foregone production of other commodities, then it makes no difference what factors are producing the commodity. Thus, the proper definition of opportunity cost saves the conclusion of classical economic theory and the free market ideal under more general assumptions. Whenever opportunity costs are known, it is possible to predict opportunities of trade. The opportunity cost principle has been employed not only in trade theories, but also in theories of production, consumption, finance, and decision making in general. It is always beneficial to reduce opportunity costs.

OPPORTUNITY COST PRINCIPLE AND THE LAW OF ONE PRICE

In particular, the opportunity cost principle has been employed to define an equilibrium condition. Depending on the specific problem statement, an equilibrium exists when there are no motives or forces to change. For individuals or larger economic units in equilibrium no opportunity costs exist. When applied to competitive markets, equilibrium prices reflect optimal resource allocation, no opportunity costs, and the Law of One Price. While such an equilibrium condition represents a *static* ideal similar to an equilibrium state in physical mechanics, competitive market equilibrium analysis in economics is based on certain critical assumptions such as:

1. Ideal competitive markets
2. Rational individuals
3. Perfect knowledge and information
4. Absence of any change
5. Perfect mobility of all factors
6. Perfect divisibility

Much of the effort in economic theory has been directed toward establishing the bounds of such idealizations by relaxing some of the restrictions and assumptions. However, it is the computational and argumentative benefits as well as the political and economic benefits, which can be gained from equilibrium models, that have made these models so popular. Over time, the free market ideal has been integrated into the value and belief structure of a large number of people and has been defended on criteria that are outside of scientific reasoning.

The Law of One Price

Given free competitive markets and perfect factor mobility, any discrepancy in resource prices creates opportunity costs which induces resource owners to move from lower paying to higher paying employment. This move continues until a single price prevails for the resource throughout the market. In equilibrium, the price of any resource will be equal to the value of its *marginal productivity* in its best alternative use. In order for an economic system to attain such an equilbrium condition, it is important that all critical assumptions hold. Stated differently, the market pricing mechanism is defined as a logical problem in which the necessary and sufficient conditions are established by the requirement to attain the desired solution. Following the analytic-deductive method of model building, the problem and the solution are defined simultaneously. Conclusions to such problem statements are then interpreted as a normative ideal that is natural. To attain the desired ideal described by the model requires that the assumptions are actually realized. This type of *normative modeling* is then used in arguments to promote the implementation of specific policies and regulations in order to replicate those assumptions implied, for example, by the classical free market ideal. Thus, the realization of normative economic theory is closely associated with political processes. Unfortunately, a reality exists that does not easily fit into the mathematical framework of ideal competitive markets.

The classical free market ideal is concerned with the state of a long-run equilibrium, which is expressed in terms of the necessary and sufficient conditions that must prevail in order to reach such a state (for example, using the theory of rational choice). Arguments are also concerned with the mechanisms and processes by which such an equilibrium state might be attained (for example, the motive to optimize or to reduce opportunity costs). Recognizing that price adjustments do not occur immediately, the Law of One Price may not hold for all resources in the *short run*. In the real world, there are costs of moving resources from one geographic area to another, and not all resources are mobile, divisible, and traded. Certain resources are fixed, at least in the short run. For example, factors that determine the plant size of a firm cannot easily be moved. However, the longer the time period considered in the analysis, the fewer resources will be fixed and the more likely will be their move to alternative uses that have higher value. Put another way, in time more resources will move to better alternative uses. On the other hand, when a resource is overpriced, in time it will be replaced by a substitute willing to receive lower payment. In a long-run equilibrium, all resources will be optimally employed, unless there are *barriers* to such adjustment processes. Furthermore, within an environment of continuous changes in technological, institutional, and physical conditions, a *continuous shift* in resource allocation will be necessary. In a free market environment, it is the response to market forces reflected in market prices and the passive reaction to such prices that will direct the shift of resources as if "guided by an invisible hand." In time and in equilibrium, a single price for all resources that are perfect substitutes will be attained in ideal competitive markets, a condition expressed by the Law of One Price.

OPPORTUNITY COST AND OPTIMAL RESOURCE ALLOCATION

The problem of optimal resource allocation within a profit-maximizing classical firm has been treated within the *marginal analysis* of microeconomics. The least cost combination of resources can be stated in terms of:

$$\frac{MPa}{Pa} = \frac{MPb}{Pb} = \ldots = \frac{MPz}{Pz}$$

where   MP = marginal productivity

P = competitive price

a, b . . . z = different resources

This statement implies that each resource will be employed until the last dollar spent on a resource adds the same amount to the total profit (value, wealth) of the firm as the last dollar spent on any other resource. A firm following this rule will not incur opportunity costs because of misallocated resources. Any deviations from such an optimum would result in an opportunity cost, which can be measured as long as the problem is fully defined and market prices are known and fixed.

A similar argument can be made for consumers who allocate their consumption spending in such a way that the marginal benefits (marginal utility) are equal to the marginal costs (competitive price), so that:

$$\frac{MUa}{Pa} = \frac{MUb}{Pb} = \ldots = \frac{MUz}{Pz}$$

where   MU = marginal utility

P = competitive price

a, b . . . z = different commodities

While this model can be viewed as based on a utility theory involving assumptions of additivity and independence as introduced by Jevons (1871) and Walras (1874), it can also be interpreted in terms of a total utility that depends on all goods consumed, which is not simply the sum of independent utilities obtained separately from each good (Edgeworth, 1881; Fisher, 1892; Tarascio, 1906).

Depending on the specific type of analysis, in microeconomics it is usually assumed that market equilibrium prices are given and fixed and that individual economic agents adjust passively to market prices by eliminating all market-related opportunity costs. This analysis does not work, however, when market participants attain marginal benefits (utilities) that differ from marginal costs.

This occurs when market participants are not atomistically equal and is discussed in terms of a consumer or producer surplus (deficit). In finance, such differences may occur with different marginal tax rates that apply to different investors. In such a case, a market equilibrium is determined by marginal market participants.

COST OF CAPITAL

A particular application of this analysis pertains to the optimal use of capital. While capital is a term with different meanings, we will consider an example of optimal land usage. Consider the case where a *society* is faced with the problem of how much land to convert to agricultural use, given the price of capital in terms of the prevailing interest rate of money. The land itself has different levels of productivity, measured in terms of the marginal productivity of capital (MPC). Thus, given that the marginal return on the land is ranked in terms of numbers, profit maximization would follow the *marginal rule*: marginal productivity of capital = marginal cost of capital or MPC = MCC.

Any restrictions would result in profit foregone or an opportunity cost. Different measures of such an opportunity cost are shown in Figure 2.1, for the case where the marginal cost of capital is known. The optimal usage of land for society is C_0, where the marginal productivity of capital is just equal to the marginal cost of capital. The term capital refers to the land as well as money, since both are freely exchangeable. In equilibrium all types of capital are employed optimally and priced at the margin.

Consider the case where an individual landowner is restricting the land use to only C_1. In this case an opportunity cost exists for the individual. Since Figure 2.1 represents marginal values, opportunity costs resulting from capital restrictions can be *measured* in three ways:

1. As the marginal productivity of the parcel of land just not put into production, or MPC_1

Figure 2.1
Opportunity Cost Measures in Optimal Resource Allocation

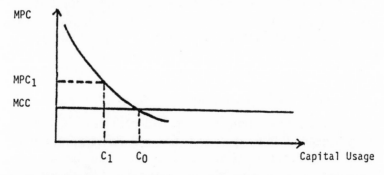

2. As the difference between the marginal productivity of capital MPC and the marginal cost of capital MCC or (MPC_1 − MCC)

3 As the difference between the optimal capital usage (C_0) and the actual capital usage (C_1) or [C_0 − C_1]

The first measure corresponds to a *marginal opportunity cost* measure. The second represents a marginal opportunity cost differential, or *relative opportunity cost*, and the third is a derivative measure expressed as the difference between actual capital use and the optimal capital use. Which of these measures is actually used depends on the specifics of the analysis. The opportunity cost can also be expressed in dollars by multiplying the quantity of land not put into service by its marginal productivity. In equilibrium, the opportunity cost should or will be equal to zero.

Consider the following example, using a single model: An individual is faced with two alternatives:

A] Invest $1000 into land with a marginal productivity of MPC = 12%

B] Invest the equivalent amount of money [V_0] in the financial market and earn an interest rate of 10% as the marginal cost of capital

Given the definition of MPC, the first alternative A] attains a value of V_A at the end of the period of:

$$V_A = V_0 (1 + MPC)$$

$$= 1,000 (1.12) = \$1,120$$

while the second alternative B] attains a value of:

$$V_B = V_0 (1 + i)$$

$$= 1,000 (1.10) = \$1,100$$

Thus, given certainty, the opportunity cost of not investing in the land can be stated as:

$$OPC = 1,120 - 1,100 = \$20$$

A similar result could be attained by using the marginal opportunity cost differential, or $MPC - MCC = 12\% - 10\% = 2\%$, so that the opportunity cost can be determined as:

$$OPC = 1,000 (MPC - MCC)$$

$$= 1,000 (.02) = \$20$$

Thus, $MPC - MCC$ gives a measure of the *relative opportunity cost* as 2%.

In equilibrium, the opportunity cost must be equal to zero. Depending on the type of argument, the adjustment mechanism to reach such an equilibrium may involve a change in the land prices, a change in the interest rate, or both or none. Land will be put into production until land usage will reach a marginal productivity equal to the marginal cost of capital. Examples of such land use expansion can be seen in the development or destruction of the rain forests in South America and the land development in Africa, plus the land use policy in the United States where farm land is converted to shopping centers and housing developments.

OPPORTUNITY COSTS AND FIXED
RESOURCES IN THE SHORT RUN

The returns paid by firms to fixed resources, such as long-term capital, are not determined by short-term considerations. Since fixed resources are not free to move into alternative employments, their short-run return is contractually settled. Depending on the *contractual arrangements,* short-term returns may be fixed or variable. Variable returns are contingent on specified events such as interest rate changes (variable rate mortgage contracts). Recognizing the wide variety of possible contractual agreements, one classification refers to obligations that must be paid (bonds) and residual ownership claims (stocks). *Ownership claims* share in the residual income that is left after all other claims have been paid. Thus, ownership claims share in the profits and losses that may accrue over time. Mobile resources must be paid the competitive amounts equal to what they could earn in alternative employment. Otherwise they would leave. This conclusion follows directly from the opportunity cost principle and rational behavior. Transaction costs may prevent a particular resource from moving away from a given employment, resulting in differences between resource payments. For example, it is quite likely that certain individuals know that they are underpaid with respect to the market, since they are not willing to move because of children in school or because of other transaction costs.

One of the fixed resources is physical capital such as plant and equipment. The original cost is allocated over the respective service life using different depreciation methods. These *depreciation methods* are specified by GAAP in accounting or by tax authorities within the tax code. Since such official allocation procedures affect periodically reported accounting income and tax payments, they are important to consider. In economic models, economic depreciation refers to the actual loss in market value or marginal productivity through physical and economic depreciation. The loss in market value can be assessed (theoretically at least) in terms of the opportunity cost principle. There are practical difficulties, however, which are associated with the problem of determining market values or opportunity costs of physical assets that are not traded. This problem is addressed by the theory of asset values.

Physical assets are bought originally with funds supplied by investors, who in return hold financial claims against those assets. Depending on the type of financial contract, we distinguish between debt and equity claims. *Debt claims* are contractual obligations that require contractual payments to holders of such contracts. While there are many different types of such agreements, traditional contracts refer to fixed income securities or bonds. *Equity claims* are ownership shares. They represent ownership rights and obligations, which depend on specific legal and institutional arrangements. Ownership claims share in residual earnings and reflect ownership risk. Single proprietors own all the ownership claims while in corporations the claims are shared and traded in stock markets. There are various institutional arrangements that specify legal provisions, public reporting requirements, and social responsibilities. While ignoring all these details, following the tradition of model simplification, we are concerned only with financial aspects of financial contracts such as bonds and stocks. Since financial claims are relatively small (infinitely divisible) and are traded in relatively competitive markets, financial markets reflect many of the necessary and sufficient assumptions required by classical economic theory and pure competitive market analysis. Thus, financial security analysis makes use of the Law of One Price and other market equilibrium criteria.

Given all the required assumptions which are a long list of idealizations that pertain to institutional arrangements, technological change, knowledge, and information as well as abilities and motives of rational investors, *specific pricing models* of financial contracts have been postulated in the relevant literature. Over time, a large number of different models have been developed reflecting different sets of assumptions and different mathematical procedures. While classical economic theory does not explicitly address the impact of modern monetary situations (they consider barter or a gold standard for money), the introduction of modern credit money introduces additional complications related to monetary policy. Some of these problems will be addressed in Part III. We are here concerned with the theory of asset values and the basic elements of the present value method to determine asset values.

THE THEORY OF ASSET VALUES AND
THE PRESENT VALUE METHOD

The theory of asset value is treated in financial market models within the framework of competitive markets, rational behavior, partial equilibrium, and the present value method. Within this framework, all economic assets are valued by their ability to generate cash flows in the future. Thus, under assumed certainty and fixed time period models any asset can be represented by a sequence of periodic cash flows that accrue to the asset over its economic life, whether it is a physical asset, a financial asset, or a human asset. While there are other assets that do not generate cash flows, such as property or art objects, a similar analysis could be applied using psychic values. Here we are only concerned with economic assets that have cash flows associated with them. Furthermore, we ignore such factors as control or power associated with ownership rights. Thus, the theory of asset value is rather specific.

Financial claims are issued by firms against physical assets they hold, which are traded in financial markets. Given that *financial markets* determine the opportunity cost of money by comparing the alternatives of investing in the market or of hoarding the money under a mattress, then markets determine the relevant interest rate associated with periodic future cash flows. By assuming perfect, complete, and free financial markets in which well-informed, atomistic investors trade, equilibrium in financial markets reflects all the requirements of ideal classical markets. In complete financial markets, all cash flow patterns offered by individual firms and different securities can be "unbundled," that is, they can be viewed as being traded separately in terms of *elementary securities*. In such a market, any pattern of cash flows can be valued in terms

of the opportunity cost principle. Thus, assets that are not directly traded are valued in terms of perfect substitutes, the Law of
One Price, and the market-given interest rate associated with the
timing, amount, and riskiness of their cash flow patterns.

The assumption of ideal financial markets adds to the assumption of classical markets the ideas that:

1. Value is associated with future periodic cash flows
2. Claims against future cash flows can be freely traded
3. All investors are fully informed and agree to given equilibrium market prices (consensus pricing)
4. Security prices reflect the present value of individual cash flow components (elementary securities)

Within such an ideal world, the equilibrium value V_0 of a sequence of future cash flows can be stated as the sum of discounted
future cash flows using the appropriate market interest rate, or:

$$V_0 = \sum_{t=1}^{\infty} \frac{CF_t}{(1 + R)^t}$$

where CF_t = periodic cash flows

R = relevant market interest rate

t = time period counter

V_0 = current equilibrium market value

While theoretically, under assumed certainty and full knowledge,
this equation determines the economic value of all assets, it is the
large number of variables involved and the large number of potential applications that has created a larger number of arguments and
alternative uses. Introducing different assumptions with respect
to the ability to know future cash flows (rational expections) and
different measures of interest rates leads to the development of
a large number of models that can be summarized by the theory
of interest rates, the theory of capital markets, and the theory of

investment. All these different theories and concepts have created a vast number of procedures and methods that attempt to forecast, predict, or manage the financial affairs of individuals, firms, organizations, and societies.

DECISION RULES

As a part of classical economic theory, the present value equation provides a possibility to measure the marginal cost of capital and the marginal productivity of capital. Different decision rules can be developed depending on particular measures and derivative measures of opportunity cost. We restrict the discussion to two examples:

1. *The Internal Rate of Return Method.* Take the example of a technical project generating the following known future cash flow pattern, after an initial cost of $1,000.

$1,000	$500	$500	$500	
0	1	2	3	time periods

Using the present value equation, it is possible to determine that R which will satisfy the equation (1), or:

$$1,000 = 500 \; \frac{1}{(1+R)} \; + \; 500 \; \frac{1}{(1+R)^2} \; + \; 500 \; \frac{1}{(1+R)^3}$$

which is about R = 23%

This number represents the marginal productivity (internal rate of return) of the project and can be compared to the relevant market interest rate or the marginal cost of capital (MCC) assumed to be 12⅓. The implied marginal opportunity cost is equal to:

$$OPC \; . \; R \; - \; MCC$$
$$. \; 23⅓ \; - \; 12⅓ \; . \; 11⅓$$

To avoid this opportunity cost, the individual should accept the project.

2. *The Net Present Value Method.* Instead of finding the internal rate of return (marginal productivity of capital), it is possible to determine the equilibrium market value of the future cash flows using the marginal cost of capital as the relevant opportunity cost of money. Using the present value equation (1), we can determine V_0, which will satisfy the following equation:

$$V_0 = 500 \; \frac{1}{(1+R)} + 500 \; \frac{1}{(1+R)^2} + 500 \; \frac{1}{(1+R)^3}$$

With R = 12%, we can determine

$$V_0 = 1,200$$

This number represents the equilibrium value of the future cash flow pattern evaluated at the prevailing market interest rate and can be compared with the actual cash outlay of 1,000 to determine the opportunity cost in $ or the net present value, as:

$$OPC = 1,200 - 1,000 = \$200$$

In equilibrium, the opportunity cost will be equal to zero, which can be stated as:

$$IRR = R$$

or

$$NPV = 0$$

The decision rules can also be shown in a graphical presentation (Figure 2.2). The internal return corresponds to the marginal productivity of capital (MPC) so that the investment criteria follow the arguments shown in Figure 2.1, as long as the cash flow patterns are well behaved. (For certain cash flow patterns multiple solutions exist.) As long as the internal rate of return is larger than the marginal cost of capital, an investment project should be undertaken. The net present value rule always results in a definite solution and is therefore preferred. As long as the net present value

Figure 2.2
Decision Rules for Investment Decisions

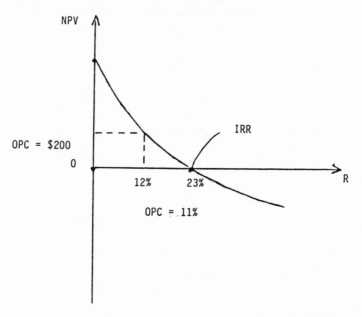

is positive, given the marginal cost of capital, the investment project should be undertaken. While variations exist in problem statements, it is the opportunity cost principle that guides rational decision making.

OPPORTUNITY COST MEASURES AND PROFIT OPTIMIZATION

The opportunity cost principle can be applied to a large number of different types of problem statements. Within a market equilibrium model, opportunity cost represents any deviation from the market equilibrium. Opportunity costs can also be measured from an optimum position. In particular, we consider here the profit optimization problem of a classical firm. The decision problem of a classical firm can be stated in terms of:

1. A goal: maximize profits
2. An objective function: profits = revenue − costs
3. Environmental conditions: that specify revenue and cost functions determined by technical consideration and fixed market prices

As a *purely mathematical statement,* the solution method of differentiation requires the existence of specific characteristics of the functions involved, whereby prices are fixed in ideal competitive markets. Furthermore, the requirement of finding only one optimal solution determines the general shape of the functions, which in retrospect are explained by diminishing returns, market saturation, and a fixed technology.

Given the problem definition and the solution technique of differentiation, the *optimization criteria* can be stated as:

maximize profit

or   marginal profit = 0

or   marginal revenue = marginal cost

A firm following this rule will not incur opportunity costs when profits are optimized. This requires that all resources are efficiently used and properly allocated, that the technology is optimal, that markets are competitive, and that no better alternative uses of resources are available.

If a firm does not follow this *optimization rule,* it will incur an opportunity cost. When mobile resources are underpaid, they will leave; when they are overpaid, the profit will be lower than necessary. When the efficiency of resource uses is low, then profits will be reduced through waste; or when the production volume is not optimal, then profits are sacrificed. In Figure 2.3, we show the effect of deviations in the production volume from its optimum (X_0). The figure shows the total profit as well as the marginal profit. The profit maximum is determined either by calculating each profit associated with different production volumes and finding the optimal point of production (full analysis) or by determining the point where marginal profit is equal to zero (marginal analysis).

Figure 2.3
Opportunity Cost Measures in Profit Maximation Model

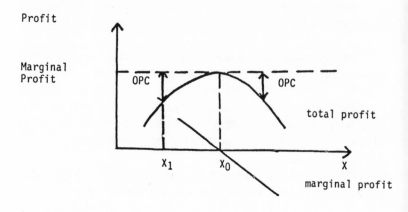

Full Analysis

The first approach or the full analysis can be viewed as a point estimation method. At each point, all benefits and costs are determined for a specific production volume, so that profits are determined by

$$\text{profits [\$]} = \text{total benefits} - \text{total costs}$$

The profit, measured in dollars, is critically dependent on the measures of costs and benefits. For example, in conventional accounting based on GAAP, costs and benefits are based only on explicit measures, whereas economic profits recognize implicit and opportunity costs, in addition. Thus, to maximize accounting profits does not imply optimal economic profits. The various point estimates are ranked corresponding to the respective production volume X in order to find the optimal profit. The optimum can be found by inspection. In this case, profits are measured in terms of dollars with respect to the reference point of zero profits.

Marginal Analysis

The second or marginal approach determines the marginal increments as profits change in response to changes in the production volume. As such, only changes in costs and benefits are recognized. As long as changes in profits are positive, production volumes should be increased until incremental profits become negative. The decision rule can be stated as

$$\Delta \text{ profits } [\$] = \Delta \text{ benefits } - \Delta \text{ cost } \geq 0$$

When changes become infinitely small, then the marginal profit optimization rule can be stated as

$$\frac{d \text{ benefits}}{dx} = \frac{d \text{ costs}}{dx}$$

or   marginal benefits = marginal costs

Both types of analysis are presented in Figure 2.3. The problem is defined within the idealized framework of complete rationality so that there is no waste and inefficiencies, no implicit costs and optimal technology. Opportunity costs exist whenever the firm is not fully optimizing.

The opportunity cost of the firm can be expressed in different ways, given that the problem statement is fully defined:

1. Within a *full analysis,* the profit at X_0 can be calculated and compared to the profit at X_1. The opportunity cost can be determined by the difference between the profits $\Pi_0 - \Pi_1$. Thus, opportunity costs can either be measured relative to the optimal profit Π_0, or in reference to zero. In either case, the optimal profit opportunity must be known. Which of the two measures is actually used depends on the type of analysis and problem statement. Opportunity costs might exist because of physical restrictions on the production capacity or because facilities are temporarily shut down during a strike or repair work, among many other reasons.

2. Within a *marginal analysis,* the marginal profit rate at X_1 can be determined and compared with the marginal profit rate at X_0 which is zero. Thus, a measure of the marginal opportunity cost is the marginal profit rate at X_1.

Since the marginal profit rate at X_0 is equal to zero, it represents a natural reference point. It should be noted that marginal rates may be negative, when the production volume is above the optimal X_0.

The opportunity cost can also be expressed in terms of number of units or as the difference between the optimal production volume X_0 and the actual production volume X_1. This measure of opportunity cost becomes easier to use and to measure in a situation where production costs and selling prices are not readily available. It represents a *practical alternative* to the other two measures. It requires, however, knowledge of the optimal production volume. This measure of opportunity cost can be used readily in attempts to control opportunity costs associated with nonoptimal production rates.

In a full equilibrium, the ratio of MPC to MCC must be equal to all other resource uses. *Linear programming* is a technique to measure the impact of different resource constraints within a multiple resource allocation model. This technique determines shadow prices, which represent the marginal opportunity cost associated with the current use of resources, as part of the solution. The total dollar impact on the profitability of the firm can be determined by multiplying the marginal opportunity cost by the number of additional units needed to reach optimality. Linear programming models can be used to study the *sensitivity of opportunity cost* to changes in constraints. An optimal solution exists when no opportunity costs exist and all resources are optimally allocated.

OPPORTUNITY COSTS AND ORDINAL RANKING

As discussed, different definitions and measures of opportunity cost exist which reflect the assumptions that specify a particular problem statement. A particular measurement of opportunity costs, as any other *cardinal measurement,* requires the determination of a reference point and a scale of measure. Formal decision models in finance and accounting use monetary units such as the dollar to measure value, profits, or costs. While this implies assumptions as to the "real" value of money in terms of purchasing power, it is common to use "nominal" money measures. In accounting this is associated with the postulate of a constant dollar value. Thus, the use of money as a unit of measure of value implies several assumptions regarding the environment in which market values are determined and in which monetary institutions control the money supply, interest rates, and inflation.

When discussing different measures of opportunity cost, it is important to address the issue of cardinal versus ordinal ranking. The theory of rational choice as used in classical economic models is concerned with the ranking of different alternatives in terms of numbers or cardinal measures of value or utility. Given that decisionmakers are able to completely rank all alternatives and that the decision requires the selection of an optimal alternative, then *cardinal ranking* is not required, however. Since any linear homogeneous value function will not alter the *relative ranking* of alternatives, value functions that are defined up to any linear transformation are sufficient to select the optimal alternative from any well-specified opportunity set. Numerical values assigned to different alternatives must only reflect a relative ranking order, instead of actual numerical values. Thus, a comparison of alternatives may be based on ordinal ranking defined up to any positive linear transformation.

For example, given that an alternative A] is preferred to alternative B], then it is possible to assign arbitrary numbers to each alternative, such that $V_A > V_B$. This value ranking does not change when one uses a linear transformation since the value relationship is retained, or

$$aV_A + b > aV_B + b$$

For selecting the optimal alternative, value functions defined up to any linear transformation are sufficient. A decisionmaker able to rank alternatives in terms of preferred or at least equally preferred alternatives can determine which alternative is optimal. A numerical measure of preference is not required. Within the framework of ordinal ranking, numerical measures of value are not required, an argument introduced by Von Neumann and Morgenstern in 1953.

The application of the *ordinal ranking principle* to decision making provides several advantages over cardinal ranking. First of all, cardinal ranking ascribes to individuals the ability to state, for example, that one alternative is twice as desirable as another. While the assumptions of complete rationality make such statements possible, it is a rather strong assumption of the abilities of decisionmakers. Cardinal measurements of *subjective values* also raise the question of whether such assigned numbers are really meaningful. Second, cardinal measures lend themselves to interpersonal comparisons, which is anathema to theorists who consider different subjective value systems. Finally, the most compelling argument against cardinal measurements of value in decision making is the fact that the assumption of ordinal ranking is sufficient to deduce major principles of economic behavior. Thus, it is unnecessary to require cardinal ranking and cardinal value functions when ordinal ranking is sufficient.

While one objective of economic theory is to explain (predict) economic behavior, another is to provide decision rules to be followed by rational decisionmakers. Within the framework of ordinal ranking, individual decisionmakers subjectively evaluate a sufficient number of alternatives of a specific problem situation using a *mental process* (possibly supported by computer programs and data files) in order to finally select one of the alternatives. Within the postulate (tautology) of rational behavior, the selected alternative will always be *optimal by definition*. Thus, an individual who is unemployed and lives in poverty reveals his or her own choice preference, given a particular choice set. The selection made from a given set of alternatives will ultimately reveal the preference of a rational individual having the freedom of choice.

As a *practical management tool,* the framework of ordinal ranking implies that individuals should be free to make their own choices. The task is not to prescribe rules to be followed in order to optimize simplified problem statements, but to provide free access to information and to give decision authority to individuals. This concept differs from the belief that control is required to encourage hired agents to perform in a prescribed way. Thus the ideal of free markets, where no individual has excessive power to affect economic decisions of others, can be applied also as a framework to be pursued *within organizations.* While this view differs drastically from traditional approaches in which organizational hierarchies are controlled from the top, the classical ideal of Adam Smith is alive and well even as a guide to establish more freedom in an organizational environment. It is the rapidly changing environment and the development of computer technology which has brought about a more participatory management style. This evolutionary change is also reflected in the Japanese management concepts of quality circle programs, Just in Time (JIT) production methods, and total quality control. While these concepts can be seen as just another fad in management, they involve a more drastic change in ideological positions.

The framework of ordinal ranking can be applied to any level of complexity since a *mental process* is dealt with instead of technical and mathematical relationships influenced by environmental conditions and artificial assumptions of a particular equilibrium condition. It is the effort to explain (descriptive or prescriptive) a particular revealed choice behavior in terms of simple mathematical models which has resulted in assumptions that include complete rationality, complete knowledge, and complete certainty. The impact of increasingly more complex problem situations on the behavior of individuals is addressed in chapter 6.

PART II

Applications of the Opportunity Cost Principle

The Opportunity Cost Principle has been defined as an integral part of classical theory that addresses the optimal allocation and the optimal use of scarce economic resources within the free market ideal. A free market economy is characterized by individual freedom of choice within a broad framework of legal and social sanctions. Consumers are free to choose among commodity offerings, producers are free to enter or exit the business of their choice, and resource owners are free to place their resources wherever employment can be found. In the marketplace exchanges will occur voluntarily and whenever it is beneficial to the individuals involved. Both profit and loss will occur as enterprises anticipate the demand for their products. Prices are determined by the free interaction between demand and supply. The market price level is seen as the guide for all economic activities of consumers, producers, and resource owners.

Classical economic theory is concerned with the *static characteristics* of a long-run equilibrium. While such a condition does not exist, it is seen as a natural state toward which a free competitive market economy will tend to move if left to its natural forces. In a long-run equilibrium all resources have moved toward optimal employment, so that no opportunity costs exist and the Law of One Price holds (macroanalysis). Individual economic entities that have not yet reached an *individual equilibrium* can use given long-run equilibrium prices to passively adjust and to reach an individual optimum (microanalysis). Since individual economic entities are small (atomistic), their individual action will not affect market prices. Only the aggregate response of a large number of market participants will change prices. Any price deviations from a long-run equilibrium price (assumed to be known) reflect *temporary imbalances* in demand and supply conditions, which provide profit opportunities that will be exploited by perceptive entrepreneurs. It is the profit motive which will eliminate temporary disequilibrium conditions. This *self-regulating mechanism* is based on individual self-interest and is seen as one of the benefits of a free market system.

The opportunity cost principle can be viewed either as a criterion to define optimality and equilibrium, or as a basis to evaluate and measure disequilibrium conditions. While classical economic analysis has been concerned with a general macroeconomic and long-run equilibrium, more recent equilibrium analysis has been applied to explain current price levels within a partial equilibrium analysis. This change in the analysis is particularly reflected in the modern theory of financial markets concerned with an *informational equilibrium* and rational expectations. Within the framework of ideal competitive markets, all prices adjust freely and swiftly to the prevailing market forces of aggregate demand and aggregate supply. An informational market equilibrium can therefore be stated in terms of the opportunity cost principle, such that "In a perfect competitive market equilibrium, the Law of One Price must prevail."

This implies, depending on the scope of the analysis, that all economic resources are optimally allocated and used perfectly efficiently or that the market reflects all available information about current and anticipated future economic conditions. Thus, the market reacts to new information about the macroeconomic environment as well as economic conditions of individual firms, which may not be operating at optimality. In equilibrium *perfect substitutes* must be selling at the same relative price. While there are other possible interpretations of market price formation and many ways to manipulate market prices, it is the belief in the conceptual ideal, besides the mathematical benefits, that has made the free competitive market concept a widely accepted method to analyze all types of problem statements.

The framework of ideal competitive markets and perfectly rational individuals entails a large number of necessary assumptions and required simplifications of a more complex reality, which have been summarized by the theory of rational choice. While strictly following the requirements set by *mathematical logic,* the competitive market ideal has been used in various applications, such as:

1. *Normative arguments,* which stress the need for a specific structure of laws, policies, and regulations with the goal to replicate the postulated assumptions in order to gain the implied benefits associated with the free market ideal

2. *Positive/scientific type models,* which attempt to explain (predict) the observed behavior of different variables and market prices or the evolution of economic/political/social entities over time

3. *Practical management procedures,* which specify decision rules and criteria to be followed in order to attain optimal solutions to specific problem statements

It is the wide variety of possible problem statements within micro- and macroeconomic models, as well as the large number of different classification methods to separate, isolate, and structure analytic problem statements, that has resulted in simple solutions and partial equilibrium models besides a vast number of methods, procedures, and arguments. In addition, it is the use of different mathematical concepts such as functional analysis, set theory, statistics, probability theory, or topology that has added to the variety of models, theories, and definitions. Recognition of the rapid evolutionary change in technology (not only in production, transportation, and data processing but also in the field of information generation, dissemination, and transmission) highlights the close interrelationship between traditionally isolated problem areas. It is the *multidimensionality* of most problem situations that must be treated within a dynamically changing world of political, economic, and social organizations. The more recently created awareness that humans are an integral part of the *natural ecosystem* of this globe has raised new questions regarding the long-run ability to survive without a more drastic change in human behavior. It is the technical ability to efficiently alter the natural environment in an effort to gain short-run individual economic benefits that, as a consequence, may alter the delicate natural equilibrium of life and life support.

By adopting and integrating the *free market ideal* into a value structure that goes beyond the economic concerns with optimal resource allocation and optimal resource usage, the free market ideal has provided a framework that promotes individual freedom, participatory government, and individual pursuit of happiness within broad confines of social and ethical bounds. It is the belief in the self-regulating mechanism of free market forces that guides the evolution of individuals and society based on individual self-interest, the profit motive, and rational behavior. This ideal defines and restricts the role of government and relies on the wisdom of individual effort to structure the laws which confine social evolution. Thus, it is the concern with values outside of the economic and scientific realm that has kept the free market ideal strong, desirable, and beneficial to many.

The application of the opportunity cost principle to *practical problem solving* introduces a number of conceptual problems. Not only are practical problem situations more complex, interrelated, and multidimensional, but the environment in which such problems exist is dynamically changing. Market prices change in response to changing conditions, so that a question exists with respect to the realization and timing of a long-run market equilibrium. While there are different arguments, it is the long-run equilibrium which is of concern to classical economic theory. It is the belief in the self-regulating natural process of free market forces that will guide human system development passively into a stable equilibrium. This view provides a basis for many arguments and a justification to search for evidence, besides attempts to predict the natural evolution of human organizations over time. In contrast to theoretical concerns that define criteria of equilibrium conditions and optimality, practical problem solving requires an objective framework to evaluate performance over time and to assess the desirability of specific conditions at any point in time.

The areas of finance and accounting are concerned with the financial aspects of economic activities resulting in costs and benefits, as well as different financial positions. *Financial consequences* are measured and reported in accounting records following prescribed procedures as determined by generally accepted accounting principles (GAAP), the Securities and Exchange Commission (SEC), and the Internal Revenue Service (IRS). As such, accounting follows a long history of financial recordkeeping in a stewardship role for owners or the public in general. Within this general view, accounting can be described as a system of procedures for setting up, maintaining, and auditing the financial records of a firm. In addition, the role of accountants includes the interpretation of those data with respect to the financial position and the financial performance. Within this role of accounting, situations arise that require the evaluation of decision alternatives, the valuation of assets, as well as the financial control of business organizations.

In contrast to accounting, the area of *financial management* becomes more difficult to define. In general, the tasks of a financial manager include activities that span from the execution of financial transactions to the planning, analysis, and control of financial strategies. As such, financial management requires the knowledge of laws, accounting procedures, data processing, and economic analysis as well as an understanding of the function of financial markets, the interpretation of financial models, and the negotiation of financial contracts. While the practical tasks of financial management may be performed by accountants, general managers, or other individuals, it is the *theory of finance* which defines the theoretical aspects of financial management within the structured ideal of classical economic equilibrium models. The function of financial management, by adopting the framework of ideal competitive markets, structured rational choice models, and microeconomic equilibrium models, is associated with the passive optimization of the market value of the firm by adjusting the firm's operation and financial structure to given market equilibrium prices. This task requires the determination of market opportunity costs, the application of the Law of One Price, as well as the evaluation of economic resource usage with respect to their relative marginal productivity. The criteria for such analysis have been introduced in Part I.

By clearly separating the *theoretical domain of finance,* concerned with market equilibrium criteria, structured optimization models, and scientific-type research, from the *practical domain of finance,* concerned with financial strategies, financial control, and practical management procedures, it is possible to recognize the limited conceptual nature of the free market ideal. Since textbooks and academic publications do not separate the two domains, the potential exists for readers to misinterpret the measurement of opportunity costs and the application of the opportunity cost principle. Recognizing the difference between the theoretical and the practical domain associated with financial management does not imply that the two can be discussed independently of each other. It is the long history of developing rational arguments, of using analytic simplifications and structured mathematical optimization models, besides the integration of the underlying value structure into rules of common sense and accepted behavior that promotes simple solutions to complex problems. Pointing to the observed economic benefits that are attributed to the free market ideal contributes to the difficulty of separating the two domains. With this in mind, the following two chapters review applications of the opportunity cost principle in finance and accounting.

3

Opportunity Cost Principle in Finance

The subject of finance is concerned with the role and function of money which is discussed in terms of a standard to measure value, a means to state financial contracts, or a specific asset to hold wealth. Over time, the definition of money has changed from pure commodity money, such as gold and silver, to pure credit money representing credit claims against monetary institutions. By recognizing the effect of the total money supply on economic activity and aggregate price levels, the government manages the money supply through monetary policies. The concern with static equilibrium models introduces the dynamics of price changes through rational expectations by which future price changes are anticipated. While classical long-run equilibrium models described an ideal state toward which an economic system develops if left to the unrestricted market forces, more recent equilibrium models in finance have adopted the view that financial markets reflect an equilibrium in the present, and that financial markets are continuously in an informational equilibrium.

To appreciate the nature of finance theory, it is important to recognize the foundation on which theoretical arguments are based.

Starting with the theory of rational choice and conditions that specify the characteristics of ideal competitive markets, a market equilibrium is determined by the aggregate supply and demand of atomistic economic units. If one applies this framework to the pricing of capital assets that are fully described by future anticipated periodic cash flows over their economic life, current capital asset prices must reflect future expected economic conditions. While this introduces a number of conceptual problems related to the uncertainty associated with future events, it has been treated purely as a matter of introducing additional idealizing assumptions. By specifying cognitive abilities of rational individuals, it is possible to assume perfect knowledge of future events or at least the ability to formulate rational expectations about future events. All these assumptions result in a large number of financial market equilibrium models that utilize different mathematical procedures and different forms of simplification.

This book does not intend to present all the different ideas, models, and arguments that are treated in the finance literature nor to account for the historical evolution of these models. Instead, we present some *fundamental principles* that underlie those arguments on which equilibrium models in finance are based. These include:

1. *The Law of One Price.* Given the necessary and sufficient assumptions about rational behavior of individual economic agents and the ideal of perfect competitive markets, any economic resource will be optimally employed (as long as they are offered in the market), and priced by the free market forces such that in equilibrium

$$\frac{MPa}{Pa} = \frac{MPb}{Pb} = \ldots \frac{MPz}{Pz} = 1$$

   where MP = marginal productivity,
   P = market price

   (Subscripts refer to different economic resources including all forms of capital.)

2. *The Opportunity Cost Principle.* Given the necessary and sufficient assumptions about rational behavior and ideal competitive markets, all economic resources will be allocated optimally and used optimally so that in a market equilibrium no opportunity costs exist. This implies also that in equilibrium economic profits are equal to zero.

While these two principles describe a general long-run market equilibrium condition, they address different aspects of the analysis, which itself depends on the scope of the problem definition. For example, a partial theory of finance is restricted to an equilibrium in financial markets, where the pricing of capital assets are fully described by future anticipated periodic cash flows over a specified time horizon. Within a *partial equilibrium analysis,* it is sufficient that cash flows are known to all market participants without requiring that all other resource markets are in equilibrium or that all resources are optimally used. All that is required is that future cash flows can be estimated and that market values reflect those cash flows with the help of the prevailing market interest rate or the opportunity cost of money. This procedure can be stated in terms of:

3. *The Present Value Method.* Given the necessary and sufficient assumptions about rational behavior and conditions describing ideal competitive markets, the current market value of future anticipated cash flow can be described by

$$V_o = \sum_{t=1}^{\infty} \frac{CF_t}{(1 + R)^t}$$

where V_o = current equilibrium market value
CF_t = periodic cash flow
R = relevant market opportunity cost of money
t = counter of time periods

This equation provides a variety of possible opportunity cost measures associated with the valuation of privately owned and non-trade capital investment opportunities (investment decision analysis) as well as procedures to analyze market equilibrium conditions. An application of this microanalysis to the wealth optimization behavior of individual economic entities provides practical management procedures and simple decision rules. As a *mathematical framework,* the present value equation provides a method to convert future expected cash flows into equivalent current values. As such, it simplifies the comparison of different cash flow patterns over time. By specifying an additive value function in terms of multiplicative value relatives (present value factors), it is possible to deduce value simply by knowing the relevant market interest rates.

4. *Value Additivity.* Given the necessary and sufficient assumptions about rational behavior, the present value method and ideal competitive markets, all values are additive as long as they are properly adjusted for the effect of time, uncertainty, and changes in the value of money.

The aggregation of value is also important for financial accounting statements which are based on generally accepted accounting principles (GAAP). There are various issues that relate to GAAP and value additivity which have resulted in calls to adopt other accounting principles based on inflation-adjusted accounting or on current value accounting to replace the accounting principles based on historical cost reporting. While different measures of value expressed in money can always be added, it is the concern with present value which is addressed in finance theory.

The theory of finance covers a wide variety of topic areas that address the economic consequences of any real or technical aspect of human behavior. As such, it is important to recognize the limitations of a financial theory that is restricted to a partial market equilibrium within a microeconomic analysis and ideal competitive markets. Given the necessary and sufficient assumptions, a perfect market economy will always be in equilibrium, as long as there are no barriers (inefficiencies) and all economic resources are perfectly mobile. While such an ideal does not exist, it provides an accepted basis to analyze economic decision making. Within a microeconomic analysis, small economic entities (individuals, firms, financial institutions) are faced with fixed equilibrium prices, to which they adjust passively in order to optimize their own financial position in terms of profit (short-term analysis) and in terms of wealth (long-term analysis). Given the appropriate assumptions, different aspects of a more complex analysis can be treated in isolation. This is expressed in terms of:

5. *The Separation Principle.* Given the necessary and sufficient assumptions about rational behavior and ideal competitive markets, different aspects of individual economic decisions can be separated and treated in isolation. This results in separate fields of specialization and a variety of subject areas that are summarized in such terms as the theory of consumption, the theory of production, and theory of investment, or the theory of finance.

While there are many applications of the separation principle, it is the nature of the analytic approach to problem simplification that has resulted in isolated subject areas and specializations, which in business organizations are reflected in departmentalization and hierarchical organizational structures.

Recognizing the impact of the separation principle, a rational individual can treat parts of more complex problem statements in isolation and optimize each aspect separately. In finance theory, this is reflected in the separation of the investment decision (valuation of capital assets), the financing decision (raising the necessary resources), and the consumption decision. An individual economic entity faced with equilibrium market prices can utilize the market information to bring its own financial position into equilibrium (optimize) by eliminating all opportunity costs with respect to the market. Thus, *privately owned* investment opportunities can be valued with respect to the market and the required resources raised as long as the respective value lies above the market equilibrium. Since all prices are competitive, and following the Law of One Price, decision making in a competitive market equilibrium is associated with optimizing market value or eliminating all opportunity costs.

Application Example 1. Given an individual with an income Y_0 and Y_1 in time t_0 and t_1, respectively. By borrowing or lending in the financial market, the individual can attain any desired consumption pattern given by the consumption opportunity set (line A–B in Figure 3.1). The slope of the consumption opportunity set is determined by the existing market interest rate at which the individual can borrow or lend. In terms of the present value method, the distance Y_0–B represents the present value of Y_1, and the distance Y_1–A represents the future value of Y_0. Which particular point on the consumption opportunity set the individual will actually select will depend on specific individual preference. All the theory states is the fact that a rational individual will select a point on the line A–B, given perfect financial markets.

While this example demonstrates the use of financial markets to shift consumption patterns in time, the analysis can also be used to demonstrate the separation principle by which capital investment decisions can be separated from consumption decisions and financing decisions, given an ideal financial market equilibrium. Consider the example of a marginal analysis where an individual is faced with different additional investment opportunities (a, b, c, d, e, f) are shown in Figure 3.2. The line E–F represents the financial market opportunity set or the capital *market equilibrium*

Figure 3.1
Consumption Opportunity Set

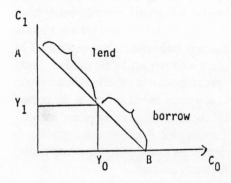

Figure 3.2
Analysis of Marginal Investment Opportunities with Capital Market Equilibrium Line (E–F)

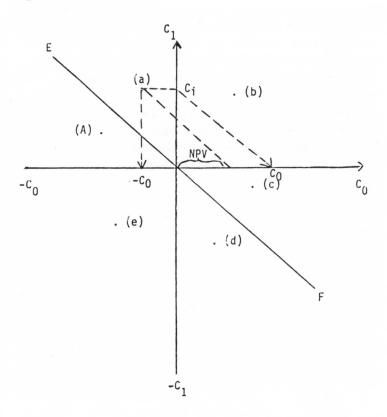

line determining the market lending and borrowing opportunities. Any opportunity below the line (E–F) is undesirable since the market line provides better oppportunities. Any opportunity above the line increases consumption possibilities to the individual. Thus, opportunities (a), (b), (c) represent better than market opportunities, while (d), (e), and (f) are dominated by the market and should therefore not be undertaken. In particular:

Alternative (a) represents a *capital investment opportunity* where current consumption is reduced and future consumption is increased. The present value of this alternative is positive. The decision to undertake this project does not depend on the consumption decision nor on the financing decision. Given perfect financial markets, the individual can borrow against the future income, repay the loan, and still retain the net present value to be consumed today or in the future.

Alternative (b) represents a *gift* which increases current and future consumption.

Alternative (c) represents a *financing opportunity* by which future consumption is pledged for current income. Since the opportunity lies above the equilibrium market line, the future value attainable by investing the money in financial markets is larger than the amount to be paid for the loan. Thus, consumption possibilities increase either in the future or today.

Alternatives (d), (e), (f) represent counterparts of the above alternatives. In the event that all alternatives are traded in the market, equilibrium prices will adjust so that all alternatives will be priced such that they will fall on the market line E–F. This result follows from the opportunity cost principle and the Law of One Price. Privately owned investment alternatives can be evaluated with respect to the market using the opportunity cost principle and the present value method, resulting in rational decision criteria.

Application Example 2. Using the underlying equilibrium principles of financial markets an individual can make a variety of other arguments. In equilibrium, all traded market alternatives must be on the market equilibrium line E–F in Figure 3.2. If they are not priced properly, *arbitrage opportunities* exist, by which individuals can make risk-free profits or receive a pure gift as presented by alternative (b). Take the case where alternative (a) is offered in the market, which is underpriced. An investor can buy the alternative (a) for $-C_0$ and borrow against C_1 to receive a pure profit, represented by the net present value or

$$NPV = C_1 \left(\frac{1}{1+R} \right) - C_0$$

Similarly, if alternative (f), which is overpriced, is offered in the market, an arbitrageur may sell the alternative short (which is possible in certain financial security markets like the stock market), receive C_0, invest C_0 in the market, and earn a larger amount at time t than is required to repay the required income on the short position (f). Thus, the arbitrageur has an increase in consumption opportunities or a free gift as presented by alternative (b).

The last transaction can also be viewed as an alternative to borrow at a better than market rate, or alternative (c). By investing these funds in the market, it is possible to gain excess profits. Such arbitrage opportunities exist until market prices adjust to an equilibrium where all opportunities are properly priced along the market equilibrium line E–F. Thus, arbitrage is a mechanism which forces markets into equilibrium. Following the opportunity cost principle or the Law of One Price, arbitrage opportunities exist whenever mispricing or disequilibrium conditions can be exploited. The problem with arbitrage in reality is related to the identification of arbitrage opportunities as well as market imperfections that permit arbitrage to occur. Such imperfections are associated with transaction costs, regulations, and the inability to sell short. Furthermore, these examples are based on certainty and full knowledge, besides other ideal assumptions.

While arbitrage positions under *uncertainty* are possible, they require more advanced financial contracts such as futures and options. Such positions do not guarantee certain success, however, but can be used to hedge specific contingencies such as unexpected price changes.

Application Example 3. The value-additivity concept allows the aggregation and disaggregation of investment opportunities. This concept is applied frequently in finance theory. For example, the total value of a firm is considered the sum of all stock values and bond values, such that

$$V_F = n_S \cdot P_S + n_B \cdot P_B$$

where V_F = total value of a firm

$$n_S = \text{number of shares outstanding}$$

$$n_B = \text{number of bonds outstanding}$$

$$P_S = \text{price of a share}$$

$$P_B = \text{price of a bond}$$

Similarly, the total value of a project can be subdivided into independent parts, which are then evaluated in isolation. The value-additivity concept guarantees that the total value must be equal to the sum of its parts or

$$V_T = \Sigma \ V_i$$

where V_T = total value

V_i = value of independent parts

While arguments exist that the total value should be larger than the sum of its parts (synergism), the *value-additivity* concept provides simple methods to evaluate projects and portfolios. The concept can be seen also as the foundation for optimizing certain components of a problem without a concern for the complex interactions among different parts. The implied independence is an accepted method in accounting and financial analysis.

RATIONAL DECISION MAKING AND THE OPPORTUNITY COST PRINCIPLE

While there are potential problems when treating a partial equilibrium in financial markets, in theoretical model building it is only a matter of making the appropriate assumptions. By being concerned only with a microeconomic analysis of small individual economic entities, we can readily assume that the *opportunity cost of money* is known and fixed in the market, however it might be determined. Similarly, we can assume that all other prices of resources are known and fixed, so that an individual economic entity can optimize its own financial position by eliminating all opportunity costs. *Optimizations* may involve such things as:

1. Eliminating all implicit costs resulting from waste, inefficiencies, wrong policies, or ineffective management procedures. In finance, this relates to the reduction of transaction costs, ineffective cash management procedures, or the reduction of tax obligations.
2. Selecting the optimal allocation of resources, so that the marginal productivity of all resources is equal to their respective market prices, and equal to each other. In finance, this relates to the investment criteria

$$MPC = MCC$$

where MPC = marginal productivity of capital measured by the internal rate of return

   MCC = marginal cost of capital determined by the market interest rate

3. Recognizing all opportunity costs of resources that are not traded This relates to the proper assessment of cash flows associated with capital usage and the pricing of resources with regard to their respective market prices as well as the opportunity cost of money.
4. Determining the optimal production output or production volume so that the periodic profits are optimized given the optimal production technology.

While the optimal resource mix, the optimal production volume, and the optimal technology are usually all interrelated and affected by dynamic changes in market prices and environmental conditions besides all other factors that describe the *multidimensionality* of practical problem situations, the use of analytic problem simplifications, separation principles, and equilibrium analysis makes it possible to reduce any complex problem situation to simple problem statements. Since no rules or limits exist that restrict the use of such simplifications, any problem situation can be simplified, structured, and optimized. After the appropriate *problem simplifications* have been applied, mathematical solution techniques can be used to discover the optimal solution. Thus, the solution technique, the problem statement, and the optimal solution are all interlinked. While this procedure creates a large number of possible problem statements and associated solutions, it is the practical relevance of such a procedure that is addressed in Part III. Here we are concerned only with simple problem statements that can be solved using the opportunity cost principle and the Law of One Price.

Consider, for example, the following problem statement: "A decisionmaker is considering the purchase of a new machine. Knowledgeable of investment decision criteria, the net present value method, and the presently prevailing market interest rate, the decisionmaker wishes to project the anticipated cash flows associated with the new machine."

Whenever the cash flows are known, the problem can be stated in terms of two alternatives:

A] Invest in the machine and gain a sequence of cash flows
B] Invest the equivalent amount of money in the financial market and earn interest income at the current market interest rate

To accept alternative A], it must have a larger present value than alternative B]. Since the present value of alternative B] is just the current amount of money to be invested (NPV = 0), it is sufficient to determine the net present value of alternative A] using the same market interest rate. As long as the NPV of the alternative A] is larger than zero, alternative A] is preferred. If one does not invest in the machine, an opportunity cost occurs relative to alternative B] or the market. A numerical example can demonstrate this point:

The machine costs $1,500

Generates annual cash flows of $500

The interest rate is 10%

The machine life is 4 years

$$NPV = \frac{500}{(1+.10)^1} + \frac{500}{(1+.10)^2} + \frac{500}{(1+.10)^3} + \frac{500}{(1+.10)^4}$$

$$- 1,500$$

$$= 84.95$$

Thus, the machine should be purchased. The alternative A] is preferred.

Most textbook examples assume that cash flows are known in order to determine the NPV figure and to apply the rational decision rule to accept or reject the project. However, consider the case where the decisionmaker is confronted with the following situations that effectively will determine the cash flow figures used in the analysis:

1. The floor space for the new machine is available since the space is currently not utilized. What is the relevant cost of using this floor space?

2. The project requires a storage facility, which is on land bought fifty years ago for an insignificant amount. What is the relevant cost of using this land?

3. Two members of the board agree to work for a nominal fee in order to see the project through. What is the relevant cost of using their services?

4. Required raw material has been stored for several years since it was purchased at a time when market prices were extremely depressed. What is the relevant cost of using that raw material?

5. If the machine operators are retrained, they can handle both the old and the new machines. What is the relevant cost of labor assigned to the new machine?

6. The firm has sufficient cash available to purchase the machine outright. The cash is currently invested in Treasury bills. What is the cost of cash associated with giving up the opportunity to earn that interest income?

While this list can be extended, it is easy to see that the decision to purchase the machine depends on a number *special circumstances*. It is the opportunity cost principle that will determine the outcome of the decision by affecting the measures of costs and benefits associated with a specific alternative. The details of the decision analysis will depend on specific circumstances introduced in the original problem statement.

Thus, it is important that a decision problem is *fully specified*. This involves, however, the specification of all other alternatives to use the money, such as purchasing a different machine or doing something else altogether. It is the assumption of an unrestricted ideal market equilibrium, in which money is freely available as long as an investment alternative has an excess market value, that makes a *partial analysis* of individual projects feasible. Without capital restrictions, all profitable alternatives should (will) be undertaken in order to optimize the market value of a firm.

COMMON TYPES OF DECISION PROBLEMS

Without going into any details, consider the case in which a decisionmaker is faced with the following alternatives:

A: a new proposal
B: an alternate new proposal
U: the currently used alternative
O: the "do-nothing" alternative
M: the market alternative

To make a *quantitative-value comparison*, it is important to identify all relevant costs and benefits associated with each alternative.

Depending on the specific comparisons, we can distinguish between absolute and relative value measures. Lacking the ability and knowledge to perform a complete decision analysis of all possible alternatives, practitioners usually restrict a decision analysis to a few alternatives such as comparing "A" and "B." These alternatives can be compared to each other, to the "do nothing" alternative "O," to the currently existing alternative "U," or to the market alternative "M," which invests the money directly in financial markets. Depending on the specifics of the analysis, we can identify various decision problems by the comparisons used or the specific reference point selected. As such, we can distinguish between the following types of decision problems that result in different opportunity cost measures:

1. *"A" is Compared to "B."* This is treated in terms of a comparison of mutually exclusive alternatives, where only the more preferred is selected. By accepting one alternative in lieu of the other, opportunity costs become the benefits of the decisionmaker. This measure of relative opportunity cost ignores the possibility that there might exist other and potentially more preferred alternatives. A decision analysis of this type is associated with dichotomies such as:

- Buy vs. lease decisions
- Make vs. buy decisions

2. *"A" is Compared to "U."* This represents a replacement-type decision. Opportunity costs exist with the currently used alternative, because it might be obsolete, inefficient, or outdated. By replacing "U" with "A," relative improvements can be made and thereby relative opportunity costs eliminated. As a partial analysis, the opportunity cost does not consider other potentially better alternatives. Examples of this type of decision analysis are associated with:

- The replacement of existing machines, projects, plants, procedures, policies, or financing arrangements

3. *"A" is Compared with "M."* These decision problems are essentially Go–No/Go decisions. By comparing individual alternatives with respect to the market, it is possible to obtain a market value estimate. It is important, however, that the market interest rate properly reflect the riskiness and time horizon involved. This relates to the idea that perfect substitutes must be selling at equal values in free markets so that appropriate substitutes must be compared. Opportunity costs exist relative to the market when profitable alternatives are not undertaken. Applications of such decision analysis can be found in:

• Security analysis concerned with detecting over- and undervalued alternatives

• Expansion or capital investment decisions of firms

• The valuation of specific investment alternatives such as real estate, business purchases, or antiques

4. *"A" is Compared to "O."* This type of comparison is the basis for measuring the absolute costs and benefits associated with a specific alternative. As long as the absolute net benefits or profits are larger than zero, the alternative is at least profitable or operating above the breakeven point. This type of decision analysis, however, does not consider market-related opportunity costs directly. Opportunity cost should be included in the analysis. Applications of such decision analysis are associated with:

• Breakeven analysis
• Accounting return on investment measures
• Internal rate of return measures

(Note: It is important to consider all applicable opportunity costs to make a correct economic decision.)

5. *"U" is Compared to "O."* This type of comparison determines the absolute costs and benefits associated with currently

existing alternatives and is usually based on accounting data. When market opportunity costs are not included, decisions based on such data may be wrong. To operate profitably it is not sufficient to identify only inefficiencies and waste. To make "optimal" decisions requires the recognition of market opportunity costs.

6. *"U" is Compared to "M."* This type of comparison determines relative costs and benefits with respect to existing market opportunities. Opportunity costs can be identified relative to the market. An existing alternative may be operating at a net profit or a positive accounting return on assets. However, compared to market opportunities, the existing alternative may carry a high opportunity cost and, therefore, should not be continued. Applications of such decision analysis are associated with:

- Go–No/Go decisions
- Product termination decisions

7. *"O" is Compared to "M."* This type of comparison studies the nature of market values. In applications to decision analysis, such studies might measure market returns, the marginal cost of capital, or the opportunity cost of money. In the literature such studies are concerned with money hoarding, cash management procedures, and theories of interest rates. Applications of such decision analysis are associated with:

- Measuring the cost of capital
- Interest rate theories
- Evaluating specific investment strategies

To apply the rules of rational decision analysis, all alternatives must be *comparable*. This requires specific means to make different alternatives comparable. For example, take the case of comparing apples to oranges. In order to compare the two alternatives, a common denominator must be used. Formal decision models use money as a common measure of value. Thus, having $200 worth of apples is preferred to having $100 worth of oranges. This statement is based on the idea that more money value is preferred to less. However, recognizing more personal preferences and the limited life of the goods involved requires additionally the *framework of markets* in which the alternatives can be freely exchanged. Thus the apples can be exchanged for $200, which then can be spent on any other goods, including the purchase of oranges. A key in this analysis is the assumption that alternatives are divisible and that individual parts are freely traded (complete markets).

VALUE RANKING AND OPPORTUNITY COST

Rational decision making in terms of value ranking is part of the tautological framework of the theory of rational choice. By neglecting psychic benefits and costs, it becomes a conceptual framework to explain average economic behavior and observed market prices within macro- and microeconomic theory. By utilizing the concept of an equilibrium determined by free market forces of aggregate demand and aggregate supply within the ideal of perfect competitive markets, we can develop a consistent economic theory founded purely on mathematical principles.

A large number of different philosophical, methodological, and ideological positions developed, following a long history of using mathematical economic models in terms of normative ideals to be implemented, as positive/scientific propositions to be tested by their ability to predict ''reality,'' as well as practical management tools to manage the affairs of economic entities (small and large). To relate practical problem solving within the practical domain of finance to the theoretical concerns treated within the domain of finance, it is important to understand the framework in which decision making has been defined within the theory of rational choice and the concepts of an ideal market environment. This is particularly important when advanced computer technology is used to solve unique decision problems utilizing specific accounting measures of costs and benefits. Besides the difficulties associated with a general lack of knowledge, with the uncertainty of predicting future events, or with the complexities involved with interrelated, multidimensional, unstructured, and dynamically changing problem situations, it is the measure of opportunity costs which ultimately will determine the outcome of a particular decision problem.

A decision analysis in which all alternatives are completely enumerated, fully defined, and perfectly comparable is known as a *complete decision analysis*. While such an analysis provides a logical basis for determining the optimal alternative, it also requires extreme abilities on the part of a decisionmaker. This ability has been associated with the term "complete rationality." A complete decision analysis must remain a theoretical framework recognizing the reality of practical decision making. Instead of a complete value ranking, a practical decisionmaker utilizes a partial decision analysis in which only a limited number of alternatives are considered and compared. This procedure can be justified by assumptions of perfect and complete competitive markets or in terms of strategic management concerns. Furthermore, in many cases decision alternatives are defined "at the margin," so that only the incremental effects on an economic entity have to be considered. For example, a decision to travel is only concerned with that particular aspect of the decision problem, even though there might be a number of other concerns including those resulting from the option not to travel at all.

The concepts of a partial and a *marginal decision analysis* are also part of classical economic theory. In particular, these concepts have been applied in finance to describe the characteristics of a capital market equilibrium. By assuming that capital markets are continuously in equilibrium reflecting rational expectations and informational efficiency, decisionmakers must properly price all traded market opportunities. Ignoring some technical assumptions about the necessary and sufficient conditions under which a market can reach such an equilibrium, any individual decisionmaker at the microlevel is faced with a fixed set of market opportunities that reflect a proper *risk-return trade-off*. Using such market information, an individual decisionmaker can value his/her own untraded, privately owned investment options as well as those of others using the opportunity cost principle. This framework implies concepts of value additivity, separation principles, economic and technical independence, divisibility, and the Law of One Price.

PREFERENCE RANKING AS AN EXPLANATORY THEORY

Rational decision making as an explanatory theory attempts to explain the observed behavior of individuals or economic entities who select specific alternatives from among a set of possible alternatives. As a proposition, rationality postulates that individuals will always elect the optimal alternative based on preference ranking of all possible alternatives. While this proposition is based on a variety of mathematical axioms and assumptions, the assignment of preference to alternatives is thought to occur through a preference function that relates specific attributes of an alternative to a single value number. While there has been considerable effort employed over time to identify such preference or utility functions, the use of monetary or dollar values to rank alternatives implies specific characteristics associated with a preference function.

Preference ranking by dollar values implies at least *ordinal preference* ranking as opposed to cardinal ranking in the sense that dollar values reflect preferences but not necessarily the strength of preferences. The underlying dollar preference function must, therefore, be at least positively sloped, and it must possess diminishing marginal preferences. In the special case where the marginal preference is constant, dollar values may reflect also a cardinal preference measure. As long as the *dollar preference function* is linear homogeneous, the resulting ranking is defined up to any positive linear transformation. This implies that a ranking order by dollar values does not change by altering the scale of measure or by changing the reference point. Thus, to explain rational decision making by ranking alternatives in dollar values, it is sufficient to postulate ordinal ranking or to assume a linear homogeneous dollar preference function.

The significance of a *linear* dollar preference function is appreciated when it is realized that linear mathematical manipulations do not change value ranking. Thus, alternatives can be ranked in terms of percentage return figures, which do not recognize the size of the total dollar investment. Furthermore, if one assumes that the underlying production functions are also linear homogeneous, the mathematics of rational decision making using dollar values becomes a simple matter of measuring dollar benefits and dollar costs associated with specific alternatives and using those money values to rank alternatives. Thus, the use of money in rational decision making becomes involved with specific measurements of costs and benefits, details of which are described by the specifics of a particular problem statement and the opportunity cost principle. While rational decision making in terms of money value ranking can be generalized, the specification of a problem statement remains very much an individual matter.

PROBLEM DEFINITION AND OPPORTUNITY COST MEASURES

While the foregoing discussion may be of little concern to practitioners who utilize accounting data instead of market data, it is important to acknowledge that *relevant* costs and benefits are associated with opportunity costs. In order to be consistent in the measurement of dollar values, it is important to use the same reference point for all alternatives. While preference ranking may not be altered by changing reference points, the measurement of costs and benefits will be affected. This is especially important when adding or subtracting dollar values to determine total profits or total wealth. Value additivity in dollars is guaranteed only when the underlying dollar-preference function is linear, and when the opportunity cost of money is properly adjusted for the impact of risk and the time horizon.

Acknowledging the *interdependence* between opportunity cost measures, the solution approach, and the problem statement itself provides insight into the reasons why the opportunity cost concept has been treated so vaguely in the literature. While investors in the market are attempting to discover opportunities to earn excess profits by eliminating existing opportunity costs, managers within firms are attempting to reduce waste and inefficiencies by discovering opportunity costs to be eliminated, and entrepreneurs too are eliminating opportunity costs by implementing new technical investment opportunities. Depending on the specifics of a problem statement, the market provides a common reference point to measure relative opportunity costs. Thus, depending on the view of how decisions *are made,* or how decisions *should be made,* the opportunity cost principle is an important element of decision analysis.

While the market equilibrium approach considers the market value as the only valid reference point to evaluate decision alternatives, managerial decisions address a more *complex reality.* In particular, many of the necessary assumptions required by the market equilibrium approach do not correspond to real world problems that are faced by practicing managers. In reality, there are many problem situations that treat decision alternatives that are indivisible, ill-structure, poorly defined, or not directly comparable. Furthermore, real world problems are frequently poorly understood, plagued by insufficient information, and placed within a dynamically changing environment. While solution methods based on mathematical rules have been applied to special situations where the required assumptions may hold, *managerial approaches* cannot afford the luxury of assuming away reality. Nonetheless, theoretical models and market-related approaches, which are discussed in Part III, do provide a framework to analyze more complex decision problems.

RISK AND UNCERTAINTY AND THE OPPORTUNITY COST OF MONEY

The critical importance of risk and uncertainty on the economic behavior of individuals and market pricing has long been recognized by economic theorists, but the tools and concepts needed for a vigorous analysis were developed only in the 1950s. For example, Irving Fisher (1930) stated, ''Our present behavior can only be affected by the expected future—not the future as it will turn out but the future as it appears to us beforehand through the veil of the unknown. . . . [R]isk means that later there may be a wide discrepancy between the actual realization and the original expectation.'' Similarly Hicks (1946) asserts, ''When risk is present people will generally act not upon the price they expect as most probable, but as if the price had been shifted a little in a direction unfavorable to them.''

While there is a continuing controversy among the academicians and practitioners of how to measure the impact of risk on prices or how to deal with the problem of uncertainty in mathematical decision analysis, over time certain concepts have been adopted, such as:

1. *The Use of Probability Theory.* Regardless of how the degree of beliefs in future events are derived, problems involving uncertainty should attach weights to prospective events that obey the laws of probability theory. In other words, personal beliefs concerning uncertain future events can be formulated in terms of subjective probabilities. (Savage, 1954)

2. *The Concept of Risk-Aversion.* Rational individuals prefer certainty and will require a compensation for bearing risk. In other word, risky alternatives require a risk premium when compared with risk-free alternatives. (Keynes, 1936)

3. *The Principle of Portfolio Pricing.* Risky alternatives are priced within a portfolio context that recognizes statistical interrelationships (covariance) among different risky alternatives, resulting in diversifiable and nondiversifiable risk measures. (Markowitz, 1952)

4. *The Separation of Risky and Risk-Free Alternatives.* Based on certain assumptions, it is possible to separate risk-free and risky investment alternatives, so that optimal proportions within a portfolio of risky and risk-free assets are independent of any particular preference functions. (Tobin, 1958)

5. *The Need for Objective Risk Measures.* Based on time series analysis of past market price changes, it is possible to derive objective

statistical measures of market risk. This concept has evolved in to a capital market equilibrium theory that recognizes statistical inter-relationships of different securities traded within a market index, resulting in an objective measure of a market price of risk. This concept is summarized by the capital asset pricing model (CAPM). (Sharpe, 1963)

6. *The Concept of Complete State Contingent Markets.* The potential outcomes of risky (uncertain) future events can be treated in terms of a large number of discrete mutually exclusive and exhaustive states of an economy. All states are well defined, and pure state contingent securities are available. A market is considered to be complete when pure state contingent securities exist for each state or when any pure state securities can be constructed from existing securities traded. (Arrow, 1964a and b)

While there are other concepts and other contributions to the development of a formal *theory of risk* and uncertainty, it is the ideal of free competitive markets and equilibrium that has provided a common framework.

The introduction of additional concepts into a well-established and structured theory requires an accommodation with other underlying principles and ideals, leading to new definitions and new interpretations. It is this adjustment process which results in potential confusion and in a potentially large number of new theories. While it is not clear what drives reality, that is, if theoretical ideals or practical needs are first, a *market response* to deal with uncertainty can be seen in the development of insurance plans and organized markets in futures, options, and options on futures. While trading in such contracts had a varied history going back to the 1800s, the recent development started in the late 1970s and the 1980s. These different types of financial contracts provide a large number of new trading strategies and hedging opportunities, as well as new pricing theories. In conjunction with the development of computer technology and instant satellite communication, the use of computer trading and large-scale information analysis besides the existence of investors of large institutions have become important aspects of modern markets. All those factors, among others, have been blamed for the market crash in October 1987.

The reason for mentioning the increasing complexity of financial markets is the increasing number of problem areas to which the opportunity cost principle can be applied. Given the notion that financial markets are continuously in equilibrium, the prevailing market interest rate can be used as a measure of the *risk-adjusted opportunity cost of money*. The basic question then relates to the particular measures of risk and their usefulness for describing market equilibrium conditions, for deriving practical decision aids, or for identifying perfect market substitutes. While this topic is beyond the scope of this book, we will discuss only specific aspects as they relate to the opportunity cost principle. It is the increasing complexity which can be interpreted as one of the reasons why the opportunity cost principle, though over 200 years old, is still a matter of controversy. In particular, we address the following issues as they relate to the opportunity cost of money: (1) the pricing of capital assets under conditions of uncertainty; and (2) the effect of financing on the risk-adjusted opportunity cost of money. While we intend to keep these discussions simple, it should be remembered that these models follow the long history of perfect competitive market ideals, the strict theory of rational choice, partial equilibrium conditions, and a consensus pricing mechanism. The impact of a more complex, interrelated, poorly defined, and unstructured environment on economic decision making is discussed in Part III.

PRICING CAPITAL ASSETS UNDER CONDITIONS OF UNCERTAINTY

In contrast to the assumption of certainty, cash streams associated with risky assets are uncertain. Within the framework of subjective probability theory, future periodic cash streams can be estimated and expressed in terms of an expected value (probability weighted average) which is discounted at the appropriate market risk-adjusted discount rate. This model can be stated in terms of the present value method as:

$$V_0 = \sum_{t=1}^{\infty} \frac{E[C\tilde{F}_t]}{(1 + R^*)^t}$$

where
V_0 = current market value
$E[CF_t]$ = expected value of future periodic cash flows
R^* = appropriate risk adjusted discount rate
t = counter of time periods

As such, nothing has really changed in the use of the present value equation. However, there is the added need to accurately estimate the expected future cash flows, since the correct valuation is critically dependent on those estimates. In a world of certainty, it is assumed that those numbers are known, given, and fixed.

To obtain the appropriate *risk-adjusted discount rate,* or the risk-adjusted opportunity cost of money, requires that the asset to be valued is compared with an equivalent perfect substitute in the market. In a world of assumed certainty and a horizontal term structure of interest rates, such concerns do not enter the analysis. The opportunity cost of money is fixed and known. With uncertainty, it is a particular set of assumptions that specify perfect substitutes and that justify the use of a particular measure of risk. As soon as a more complex reality is recognized, the practical value of any simplified model becomes questionable. While there are different models to determine a risk-adjusted discount rate, it is the *capital asset pricing model* that determines the relevant risk with respect to the market following statistical estimation procedures. Within this framework, the risk-adjusted market discount rate can be written as:

$$R^* = R_F + [E(R_m) - R_F] \cdot \beta$$

with
R^* = the risk-adjusted discount rate
R_F = the risk-free rate
$E(R_m)$ = the expected market rate of return
β = a statistical measure of market risk

To utilize this equation to determine the risk-adjusted opportunity cost of money, it is important that the variables be properly estimated and that the asset to be valued has the same market risk assessment. While there are practical limitations to this model, it does provide an objective measure to treat the impact of risk and uncertainty, as long as all numbers are properly known. As a numerical example, consider the following case:

A decisionmaker has the following two investment alternatives:

A] invest into a physical project with expected periodic cash flows $E[CF_t] = \$500$ over the next four periods. The project costs $1,500.

B] invest directly into the capital market into an equivalent perfect substitute which has an expected return of 10%.

Essentially this problem statement is analogous to the problem under certainty, except that the risk-adjusted opportunity cost of money is calculated based on the following estimates:

$$R_f = 5\%$$

$$E[R_m] = 16\%$$

$$\beta = .46\%$$

such that $R^* = 5\% + (16\% - 5\%) .46 = 10\%$

The Net Present Value then becomes

$$NPV = \frac{500}{(1+.10)} + \frac{500}{(1+.10)^2} + \frac{500}{(1+.10)^3} + \frac{500}{(1+.10)^4}$$
$$- 1,500$$

$$= 84.95$$

Since the risk-adjusted net present value is larger than zero, project A] is preferred to B]. It is the opportunity cost principle and the Law of One Price that determine the preference within the framework of rational behavior. The equivalent risk-adjusted discount rate is determined in the market for an equivalent perfect substitute already traded. Therefore the difficulty is to detect proper market substitutes for evaluating nontraded investment alternatives.

THE EFFECT OF FINANCING ON THE RISK-ADJUSTED OPPORTUNITY COST OF MONEY

This subject has been controversial and is addressed in terms of the *Independence Proposition* (Modigliani and Miller, 1958) or the Law of Conservation of Value (Williams, 1938). The argument addresses the question of what the market actually values, or the postulate that the combined market value of a firm's securities is invariant to the mixture of bonds and stocks used to finance the firm's asset holdings.

While there are various forms of this argument, under ideal competitive market assumptions where individuals are free to select any combination of securities and can borrow at the same rate as the firm, it can be shown that individual investors can *replicate* any mixture of bonds and stocks independently of the particular mixture selected by a firm. Thus, in equilibrium the market value of a firm must be independent of its financing decision. Essentially what this argument states is the postulate that in complete markets a levered firm and an unlevered firm are perfect substitutes, as long as the future pattern of cash flows falls into the same risk-class. Thus, markets price cash streams accruing to real assets, and it does not matter how they are divided by different financing arrangements.

The consequences of this argument, which is based on a number of idealizing assumptions, can be stated in terms of the following propositions:

1. The equilibrium market value of a firm is independent of any particular financing arrangements (value additivity)

2. Risky cash streams can be evaluated with the help of the risk-adjustment market opportunity cost of money associated with perfect substitutes (Law of One Price)

3. The expected market return on risky assets reflects the appropriate market price of risk (no arbitrage opportunities)

4. To earn higher rates of return in the market requires the exposure to higher levels of risk (risk-aversion)

5. A market equilibrium reflects the appropriate risk-adjusted rate of return (opportunity cost principle)

While these propositions provide for a large number of examples and applications, the underlying principles are based on a perfect competitive market equilibrium, which is described by the opportunity cost principle and the Law of One Price.

4

The Opportunity Cost Principle and Accounting

Model building is not only a scientific method for determining scientific truth or a logical procedure for dealing with interrelated and complex problems, but also a necessary practice to cope with an otherwise confusing world. By utilizing metaphors, analogies, and models, it is possible to describe poorly understood problem situations based on commonly accepted beliefs. Thus, model building can be seen as a necessary procedure for individuals to communicate and to explain their surroundings, their activities, and their goals and values.

In contrast to theoretical models developed in finance and economics, based on postulates of rational choice and ideal market equilibria, *accounting principles* evolved over a long history of recording business-related information. Most likely dating back to early tax-collecting procedures and the desire to keep records of ownership, discussions about the benefits of double-entry bookkeeping were published as early as 1494. Modern accounting techniques evolved largely in response to specific needs and changes in the socioeconomic environment. In general, accounting procedures can be viewed as a set of techniques that are considered to be useful and that have been accepted by the profession because of their alleged logical conformity with *generally accepted accounting principles* (GAAP). Since no one generally accepted accounting theory exists, changes in accounting principles occur mainly in response to emerging problems and attempts to formulate acceptable solutions. When a specific accounting theory fails to produce desired results, it is replaced by one which provides the necessary logical framework.

The process by which accounting principles have evolved has changed over time. In the early part of this century, management had almost full control over the methods by which accounting information was collected and the type of information that was reported. As a consequence, different firms adopted different accounting techniques to accomplish similar objectives. One of the main interests focused on the determination of taxable income. Largely in response to the stock market crash in 1929, government intervention resulted from the Securities Acts of 1933 and 1934. From 1959 to 1973, the American Institute of Certified Public Accountants (AICPA), through the Accounting Principles Board (APB), started to publish opinions with the goal of codifying acceptable accounting techniques and eliminating undesirable accounting procedures. Even though they did not rely on any particular theoretical framework, these opinions developed a set of generally accepted accounting principles. This *authoritarian approach* developed accounting techniques that relied on pragmatic solutions with the goal to maintain the basic two accounting equations, namely the balance sheet and accounting profit equation. The *balance sheet equation* is usually stated as:

$$\text{Assets} = \text{liability} + \text{owners' equity}$$

and the *accounting income equation* as:

$$\text{Accounting income} = \text{revenues} - \text{costs}$$

These two equations imply a number of concepts or accounting principles that relate to specific underlying assumptions, methods, and postulates that specify the nature, components, and measures of specific accounts. A general dissatisfaction with the authoritarian approach resulted from abuses of accounting reports which either neglected much of the important information or presented it in footnotes. The increased complexity of financial contracts created a whole array of "off-balance sheet" financing arrangements, so that the value of accounting information became increasingly suspect.

The recognition that the lack of a comprehensive theory of accounting will continue to undermine public confidence in accounting reports, not to mention the fact that accounting numbers do affect economic behavior, has led to the *politicization* of the accounting standard-setting process. The Financial Accounting Standards Board (FASB) replaced the Accounting Principles Board (APB) in 1973. While there are various reasons that have been brought forth to explain this change, in 1971 two study groups were created by the AICPA. The first group, known as the Wheat Committee, was charged with the task of improving the accounting standard-setting process. The report led directly to the formation of the FASB. The second group, known as the Trueblood Committee, was charged with the development of the objectives of financial statements, and in particular with determining: (1) who needs financial statements; (2) what information is needed; (3) how much information can be provided by accounting; and (4) what framework is required to provide the needed information. Although the Trueblood Report (1973) addressed a multitude of issues, its implementation involved many problems and concerns, which the FASB has subsequently considered. With respect to the user's need for accounting information, the FASB set forth the qualitative characteristics of financial statements in *Statement of Financial Accounting Concepts No. 2* (1980), including: relevance, reliability, neutrality, comparability, and materiality. Whatever the approaches and methods used to formulate a conceptual framework of accounting, to measure and report accounting information, and to utilize accounting information, it is the set of GAAP that has governed the development of accounting techniques.

ACCOUNTING POSTULATES AND ACCOUNTING PRINCIPLES

While much has been written in the accounting literature about accounting principles, postulates, and theoretical concepts, the lack of a unifying framework leaves the potential for misinterpretations and divergent points of view. Despite these problems, which exist similarly in other fields, there are some *basic postulates* that underlie accounting information:

1. *The Entity Postulate.* This postulate holds that each enterprise is a separate and distinct entity, which stands apart from its owners and other firms. This defines the area of concern to accountants and limits the number and types of transactions to be reported. The entity concept applies, for example, to partnerships, sole proprietorships, and corporations. While accounting concentrates on financial aspects of economic transactions, there are different ways to define an accounting entity. This may start with legal definitions, economic interest, or management control and continue to aspects of information generated in terms of security pricing, socioeconomic responsibility, financial forecasting, and human resource accounting.

2. *The Going Concern Postulate.* This postulate holds that a business entity will continue to operate, so that financial statements provide only a tentative view of the financial situation of a firm as part of a series of continuing reports. As such, this postulate justifies the valuation of assets on a nonliquidation basis and provides the foundation for depreciation accounting. Because neither current value nor liquidation or replacement value are reported, the postulate calls for the use of historical cost accounting.

3. *The Money Unit of Measure Postulate.* This postulate implies two principal limitations of accounting information. By concentrating on measures related to transactions, accounting information is expressed in monetary units. Thus, financial statements do not report other relevant but nonmonetary information. This leads to the definition of accounting information only in terms of quantitative, numerical, and past-related events and ignores more

qualitative and future-related information, besides other measures such as units of production or units in inventory. Furthermore, by concentrating on nominal money measures, instead of inflation-adjusted measures that reflect purchasing power changes, accounting information reflects a stable monetary unit of measure. This allows for simple-value additivity, but is vulnerable to criticism especially when inflation becomes an important element in economic decision making.

4. *The Accounting Period Postulate.* This postulate holds that financial reports depicting changes in the financial position of the firm should be reported periodically by selecting annual periods. The use of fixed reporting periods requires the determination of accruals and deferrals, which is a principal difference between accrual accounting and cash accounting.

Besides these basic accounting postulates, which define the underlying conditions under which accounting reports are prepared, a variety of *accounting principles* exist that call for specific techniques, procedures, and characteristics of reported accounting information. As such, accounting procedures reflect the requirements set forth in GAAP. The following GAAP should highlight the nature of accounting information:

1. *The Cost Principle.* According to this principle, historical acquisition cost is the appropriate basis for recognizing costs. This implies that all items are valued at the exchange price at the date of acquisition.

2. *The Revenue Principle.* This principle specifies the nature and components of revenue as well as the timing and measurement. While a variety of possible issues and definitions exist that depend on the type of business activity and the type of contractual agreements, this principle specifies the crucial events and procedures that result in accounting income. These procedures may not necessarily correspond to tax laws or requirements set by the SEC.

3. *The Matching Principle.* This principle holds that expenses should be recognized in the same period as the associated revenues in order to determine accounting profits. This implies that costs

associated with the use of long-term assets are written off over time (e.g., depreciation) and that expenditures which are incurred during the same time period and are not directly associated with the revenue are "expensed" unless it can be shown that they are related to future benefits. The matching principle gives rise to a number of accounting issues, the treatment of which depends on specific business situations.

4. *The Objectivity Principle.* This principle relates to the verifiability of accounting measurement procedures and the usefulness of accounting information.

5. *The Consistency Principle.* This principle implies that the same accounting procedures will be used for similar conditions and not be changed at will. The application of this principle makes financial statements more comparable from period to period.

6. *The Full Disclosure Principle.* This principle requires that financial statements be prepared in accordance with GAAP and that economic events be adequately represented. Full disclosure implies that no information of substance will be omitted or concealed.

7. *The Conservatism Principle.* This principle acts as a constraint on the presentation of accounting information. It implies that when someone is choosing from among different acceptable accounting techniques, preference should be given to those that have the least favorable impact on stockholders' equity.

8. *The Materiality Principle.* This principle acts as a justification for exceptions and modifications. As such, the principle holds that transactions that have insignificant economic impact may be handled in an expeditious manner. That is, they may not be disclosed, whether or not in conformity with GAAP. This principle provides guidance to the accountant when deciding what should be disclosed in a financial report. Thus, it gives accountants the opportunity to decide what is of relevance to particular areas of accounting information.

9. *The Uniformity and Comparability Principle.* While the consistency principle refers to the use of the same accounting procedures for a firm over time, the uniformity principle refers to

the application of the same accounting procedures among different firms. The objective of this principle is the reduction of diversity among different accounting procedures used by firms to achieve comparability between financial statements. This principle is controversial and various positions exist that argue for and against uniformity.

ACCOUNTING PROFIT VS. ECONOMIC PROFIT

After having reached some insight into the general nature of accounting information, we address the use of the opportunity cost principle in the preparation of accounting information as well as in the use of accounting information. At the outset it is important to recognize the difference between accounting data and economic theory. To demonstate this difference, we present the following example:

Let us take a small business that sells a product. The financial condition has been prepared by an accountant, recognizing only explicit costs as shown in Exhibit 4.1. The form of the business, shown here as a corporation, is a matter of importance. The total income to the owner is salary + income = $9,200, on which personal taxes, in addition to corporate taxes, have to be paid as long as all income is distributed as dividends.

Exhibit 4.1
Accounting Income of a Small Business for a Specific Time Period

Total revenue		$15,000
Less cost of:		
Goods sold	2,800	
Rent	3,000	
Salary	4,000	
	9,800	
Total		9,800
Accounting Income		5,200

Now let us consider an analysis that recognizes *opportunity costs*. Suppose that the land which rents for $3,000 could be re-rented for $5,000. In addition, suppose that the salary that could have been earned by the owner by working in some other place would have been $7,200 instead of the $4,000 paid. The total opportunity costs of land and labor could be viewed as $5,000 and $7,200, respectively. These opportunity costs should be recognized in a decision about whether the business should be continued. The calculations are shown in Exhibit 4.2.

As seen in column A, the proper market price for the land and labor are used, so that the economic income is zero. All resources are properly priced reflecting an *equilibrium condition*. If, for example, as shown in column B, the employment potential would have been $15,000, an economic loss of $7,800 would have occurred. A conclusion could be to close the business, re-rent the land, and take the job for $15,000. On the other hand, if the opportunity cost for labor would be just $4,000, which could be earned somewhere else, then the $3,200 represents pure economic income, which reflects the proper payment of all resources at the prevailing market price. As others see that economic income can be made, they can be expected to move into the industry to take a share of that *excess income*. Of course, most entrepreneurs would like to earn more than their opportunity costs, plus any psychic benefits that can be gained from working for themselves.

As a conclusion to this example, it can be stated that economic decision making should recognize the opportunity costs of resources

Exhibit 4.2
A Comparison of Economic Income under Three Alternatives

	A	B	C
Total Revenue	15,000	15,000	15,000
Cost of goods sold	2,800	2,800	2,800
Rent	5,000	5,000	5,000
Salary	7,200	15,000	4,000
Total Cost	15,000	22,800	11,800
Economic Profit	0	-7,800	+3,200

used. By having a special deal or by ignoring the implicit costs of certain resources, an individual can earn an accounting profit, even though the economic profit might be negative.

The analysis of the above example was based on total costs during a specified time period. Similarly, the analysis could be made with marginal costs such as the cost of land per week or the cost of labor per hour. Also, the opportunity costs could reflect different measures. For example, the incremental opportunity cost of land is $5,000 − $3,000 or $2,000, and the incremental opportunity cost of labor would be $7,200 − $4,000 = $3,200 (Example A). The sum of *incremental opportunity costs* is equal to $5,200, which represents the amount by which accounting income is overstated. Similarly, the comparison can be made between examples, resulting in incremental economic profits. For example, the incremental profit between Examples A and C is equal to $3,200, reflecting the lower opportunity cost of labor. As a conclusion, we can state that the calculation used to reach a specific comparison depends on the type of analysis used, which also determines the specific measure of opportunity costs.

THE OBJECTIVE OF ACCOUNTING

The above example should have clarified the difference between accounting information and an economic analysis that includes opportunity costs. Accounting information, by following the principles and postulates that are summarized by GAAP, is essentially concerned with verifiable cost data and the adherence to the basic accounting equations. Thus, accounting measures traditionally emphasize form over substance. More recently there has been an attempt to formulate the objective of financial accounting data with respect to their use, emphasizing substance over form.

For example, *Statement of Financial Accounting Concepts No. 1* (1978) asserts that the central objective of financial accounting is "to provide information to help present and potential investors and creditors and other users in assessing the amounts, timing, and uncertainty of the prospective cash receipts from dividends or interest and the proceeds from the sale, redemption, or maturity of securities or loans.'' The FASB recognizes that the reason for supplying this type of accounting information lies in the postulated nature of users and their assumed analysis in terms of the present value method: ''Since investors' and creditors' cash flows are related to enterprise cash flows, financial reporting should provide information to help investors, creditors, and others assess the amounts, timing, and related uncertainty of prospective net cash inflows to the enterprise.''

Thus, both the objective of accounting information and the function of financial management are cast into the same theoretical framework. The FASB, recognizing that it is unknown how accounting data are used by specific users to estimate future cash flows, stated that:

> Investors, creditors, and others may use reported earnings and information about the elements of financial statements in various ways to assess the prospects for cash flows. They may wish, for example, to evaluate management's performance, estimate earning power, predict future earnings, assess risk, or to confirm change, or reflect earlier predictions or assessments. Although financial reporting should provide basic information to aid them, they do their own evaluating, estimating, predicting, assessing, confirming, changing or reflecting.

Essentially, what this statement highlights is the difference between theoretical concepts and practical applications. While this differentiation is important, the terms and definitions used in the field do not clearly separate the two.

The FASB, in its *Statement of Financial Accounting Concepts No 1,* also asserts that: ''Financial reporting is intended to provide information that is useful in making business and economic decisions for making reasoned choices among alternatives used of scarce resources.'' This objective of financial accounting addresses the use of accounting information in forecasting long-run cash flows and in assessing their amounts, timing, and uncertainties. This implies that users of financial accounting data are concerned with economic value derived from the present value model in conjunction with accounting information. Assuming the use of such a valuation approach, the FASB does not call for any particular data that would assist users in this valuation effort. Instead, the statement suggests: Information provided *should* be useful—emphasizing the importance of cash to people and the activities they use to increase the productive resources and outputs of goods and services in an economy—rather than the kinds of information that *may be* useful for that purpose.

In conventional financial accounting, in view of the emphasis on verifiability and historical cost, there is no consideration of revenue foregone. No attempt is made to reflect alternatives not taken. The cost of using an asset, for example, equipment, should be the greatest amount that could be obtained from utilizing this asset in an alternative way. That is not considered in accounting, however. The *current replacement cost* or exit value (i.e., nondistress liquidation value) of an asset can be viewed as an opportunity cost, but disclosure of such nonhistorical cost data is currently voluntary, which means that it is not done. Opportunity costs are not recorded by accountants since they do not entail cash outlay costs.

The National Association of Accountants (NAA), in its *Statement No. 1A* "Definition of Management Accounting" (1981), states:

> Management accounting is the process of identification, measurement, accumulation, analysis, preparation, interpretation, and communication of financial information used by management to plan, evaluate, and control within an organization and to assure appropriate use of and accountability for its resources. Management accounting also comprises the preparation of financial reports for nonmanagement groups such as shareholders, creditors, regulatory agencies, and tax authorities.

While the FASB is concerned with financial accounting, the NAA is concerned with managerial accounting. The definitions of accounting by the FASB and the NAA reflect the change from the traditional result-orientation to the more recent process-orientation of management. In essence, accounting has a dual role in business management. The first role relates to the internal management of a firm, which is associated with managerial accounting procedures. The information collected should enhance the internal control of operations with the aim of increasing efficiency by reducing waste and losses. The second role of accounting relates to the function of recordkeeping, the measurement of periodic operating performance, and the reporting of financial positions in terms of income and value. The information collected should assist external investors and creditors in assessing the financial position of the firm.

When considering costs, benefits, profits, and losses, people commonly think about cash flows or accounting definitions. Since accounting information is primarily concerned with the measurement of income based on explicit costs and benefits of objectively determinable transactions during a specified reporting period, implicit costs and opportunity costs are not recognized. Thus, accounting income *does not* represent economic income. This special characteristic of accounting data must be recognized when such data are used in any economic analysis.

The significance of this *informational deficiency* is important when accounting data are used to make decisions. To make a suitable decision, individuals must adjust accounting information. By ignoring opportunity costs and implicit costs, they will likely make the wrong decisions and therefore select nonoptimal alternatives. On the other hand, actual decisions may reflect not only accounting data, but also a whole realm of future projections including risk-analysis and opportunity cost considerations. In such a scenario, the role of accountants and the value of accounting information may be seen in a different perspective. Accountants record the consequences of decisions made by individual decisionmakers. Accountants provide information that reflects the consequences of past decisions. Thus, accountants should not be concerned with theories that particular decisionmakers may use to deal with accounting information, nor with economic models that attempt to explain economic behavior. Instead, accountants should be concerned with providing relevant and reliable accounting information.

THE OPPORTUNITY COST PRINCIPLE AND THE USE OF ACCOUNTING INFORMATION

Accounting has a long-standing reputation as being the principal information discipline in business, providing the necessary information for a wide variety of decisions, which include such problems as:

1. Should a firm be bought and, if so, at what price?
2. How should the purchase be financed?
3. What is the time schedule to repay borrowed funds?
4. What additional sales outlets should be developed to market the new products?
5. Which new product lines should be emphasized or discontinued?
6. How should the firm's financial information system be designed for the planning and control of the business and the reporting of financial results?

The foregoing list can easily be extended to include many other decision problems that require accurate and timely business information. On a more theoretical level, accounting seeks to provide useful information about assets, resources, and income streams in order to:

1. Allocate resources among alternative uses
2. Control the efficient use of resources
3. Report on the financial position to creditors, owners, governments, and the general public
4. Aid in the accomplishment of social goals

While these objectives for the use of accounting information follow directly from the ideals associated with economic theory, accounting does not address the type of information required to accomplish those objectives. For example:

- To allocate resources optimally requires opportunity cost measures
- To control the efficient use of resources requires implicit cost measures
- To report meaningful financial positions requires current information
- To aid in the accomplishment of social goals requires relevant information

In each of these areas, *traditional* accounting information based on GAAP falls far short of what is needed. In addition, most cost accounting systems or internal management accounting systems address accounting definitions of costs and benefits in order to fulfill the postulates and principles of accounting information. Thus, to accomplish the goals set for the use of accounting information as outlined above requires the recognition of broader issues and more complex problem stituations.

When considering the implications of the *opportunity cost principle* for the use of accounting information in decision making, it is important to recognize the theoretical framework in which this principle has been defined. Starting with the fundamental principle of rational behavior as a matter of tautology, individuals will always select the optimally preferred choice alternative, as long as they are free to do so. While this postulate can be used to justify specific types of models and specific mathematical procedures, originally it implied subjective valuations and psychic values. A rational individual will gather the necessary information to make rational decisions, which may include accounting data if they are relevant. The framework of ideal competitive markets and a market equilibrium does not alter this fundamental principle of rational behavior. Free individuals will trade as long as it is beneficial to them and as long as they have resources to trade. A market equilibrium is reached through the free interaction of individuals. The extension of this simple idea to state mathematical optimization procedures that explain market equilibrium conditions with the aid of accounting information and structured mathematical models introduced a variety of rather specific and necessary assumptions. As such, these assumptions reflect the requirements of mathematical procedures that define a specific type of rationality.

By adopting the framework of microeconomic and a partial market equilibrium to predict economic behavior, rational decision models, based on mathematical procedures and objective measurements, became an important element in the area of scientific management. By researchers' extending the scientific quest to discover natural laws governing economic behavior, the belief in a deterministic equilibrium found its way also into accounting research. Business data provided by accounting procedures was seen as the information necessary for all the required decisions. This basic view changed when it was realized that accounting data had serious shortcomings in a dynamically changing world with continuous inflationary price changes.

As a criterion to describe a market equilibrium, the opportunity cost principle provides a measure to evaluate *disequilibrium* conditions. As such, opportunity costs provide the basis for decision making. In a long-run equilibrium, defined for perfect competitive markets, all opportunity costs are zero, the Law of One Price holds, and all economic profits are zero. Any deviation from such an equilibrium provides risk-free arbitrage opportunities that will be exploited as long as there are no barriers that prevent such activities. It is this continuous process that brings markets into equilibrium, which provides new investment opportunities and which keeps a dynamic economic system developing. To reduce opportunity costs requires, however, that relevant information is available to assess decision alternatives. The fact that traditional accounting information does not convey this is a problem to those who want useful information for decision making.

The opportunity cost principle in practical decision making provides a method to evaluate problem situations that occur because of nonoptimal conditions. These problem areas may not be restricted to measures of accounting profits and explicit costs, but may relate to implicit costs and psychic values. In this sense, *nonoptimality* may relate to much broader concepts than those defined for rational economic behavior based on explicit market values. By broadening the scope of a problem analysis, it is possible to discover inter-relationships and complex adjustment processes that in time may eliminate current problem situations. Such dynamic processes are not "obvious" in traditional analytic, static, and simplified models. It is this concept that is addressed in Part III.

The opportunity cost principle also provides criteria for the selection of relevant information for economic decision making. Depending on the particular decision problem, this may include accounting data besides measures of intrinsic and opportunity costs. Inasmuch as decisions are future-related, this involves the concept of environmental stability. Within short-term decision problems in which the environment and prices do not change, accounting data may well provide relevant information. Consider, for example, the following types of economic problem situations:

1. *Nonoptimal Resource Allocation.* Example: A repair shop provides internal services that can be attained also externally.

a. The decision of whether or not to replace the service emphasizes future costs. All past costs for the old machines are sunk and thus irrelevant in the replacement decision. The relevant items are future costs and the expected disposal value of the old machines.

b. The make-or-buy decision generally hinges on the utilization of vacated facilities if the buy option is selected. The question is whether the facilities under consideration can be used in some alternative manner. If so, there is an opportunity cost associated with alternative uses.

c. In the buy-versus-lease decision, the relevant costs are expected future cost differentials between the two options. Costs that are expected to be the same under both alternatives are irrelevant.

2. *Nonefficient Resource Use.* Example: Measures of standard costs vs. actual costs. Inasmuch as these problem statements address explicit costs only, it is the accumulated cost accounting information which is relevant for the analysis of waste and inefficiencies. The determination of standard costs and actual costs require clear measurement criteria to perform an accurate variance analysis.

3. *Nonoptimal Policies.* Example: The implicit costs of lost sales. Besides the explicit loss of sales there is potential goodwill lost when a firm loses a prospective customer. This may include the lost customer as well as the loss of potential future customers who know the customer. Traditional cost accounting systems fail to reflect such implicit costs or opportunity costs because they are difficult to quantify objectively.

4. *Ineffective Policies.* Example: Wrong marketing strategies. This may include the cost of not reaching the desired target customers as well as the cost of a wrong product design. An analysis based solely on explicit costs of the marketing program would not be sufficient. It is the implicit cost as an opportunity cost which determines the relevant decisions.

5. *Constraints on Reaching a Better Alternative.* Example: Operating at limited capacity because of resource constraints. Given that specific resource limitations restrict the operating capacity, it is not the explicit cost of the resources but the opportunity cost of not operating at full capacity which determines the relevant information for decision making. Thus, a missing bolt, costing $1, may be associated with an opportunity cost of thousands of dollars.

While there are other examples that demonstrate the limitation of traditional accounting data for decision making, we consider here the case of transfer pricing. A *transfer price* measures the effects of intrafirm transactions in which one profit or investment center buys its inputs from or sells its outputs to another center in the firm. As such, transfer prices reflect an opportunity cost of internal transfers. When transfer prices are not properly established, a profit center manager is not able to make decisions that are optimal for the firm as a whole. The predominant feeling is that the best transfer price is a market price or some version of a market price, to the extent a market exists for the intermediate product. The application of a market price in transfer pricing helps to guard against transfer prices that fall below the opportunity cost of the selling division.

If the selling division can sell all it can produce (i.e., full capacity) to external customers, then the opportunity cost of that division is the purchase price that the external customers are willing to pay. In this case, the transfer price in the firm should not be lower than the market opportunity cost, reduced by any costs avoided due to inside sales. Otherwise the selling division and the firm as a whole may suffer real losses.

In the case of a selling division having excess capacity, the opportunity cost may not be the market price. It can be argued that excess capacity calls for negotiations of transfer prices below the market price. As long as the selling division receives more than its short-run variable cost, that division benefits. If the selling division has excess capacity and the buying division buys from an external supplier, then there will be less than optimal results for the selling division as well as the firm as a whole.

An example where different opportunity cost measures lead to different conclusions is associated with the residual income approach to evaluate the performance of *investment centers*. The residual income represents the excess of operating income over the imputed interest paid on capital invested, and it is based on accounting conventions. The imputed interest should reflect the current market opportunity cost instead of historical costs. The use of residual income measures to evaluate the performance of an investment center may well lead to inappropriate decisions when current market conditions are ignored.

THE OPPORTUNITY COST PRINCIPLE AND THE REPORTING OF ACCOUNTING INFORMATION

Financial accounting, by adhering to the two basic accounting equations, follows two positions concerned either with the balance sheet and the fair representation of financial position or with the income statement and the fair measure of accounting income. Inasmuch as the two positions lead to conflicting accounting measures, compromises have been made. These compromises relate also to the use of the opportunity cost principle in the preparation of financial reports. For example, *conventional accounting income* was not concerned with unrealized gains or losses that arise from the holding of investment assets until FASB *Statement No. 12*, "Accounting for Certain Marketable Securities" (1975), was issued on this subject. Under this statement, both the current asset and long-term investment portfolios of marketable equity securities are priced at the end of each financial reporting period to reflect the lower of the portfolio cost and market. *Writedowns to market* are reflected as unrealized holding losses. They are shown in the income statement for short-term holdings of marketable equity securities and in stockholders' equity for long-term holdings of marketable equity securities. *Writeups to the original cost,* but not above, are called for when the portfolio market value subsequently exceeds the portfolio cost. Such writeups constitute unrealized holding gains, shown in the income statement for current asset holdings while directly in stockholders' equity for long-term asset holdings.

Other situations where financial accounting information utilizes specific aspects of the opportunity cost principle, are associated with:

1. *Inventory Valuation.* Using the lower of cost or market method is somewhat like the treatment of marketable equity securities. The lower of cost or market approach is applied to inventories and unrealized holding losses are recognized for financial accounting and reporting purposes. Unrealized gains, however, are not reflected in financial statements because inventory, in contrast to marketable equity securities, is written down to reflect not only price declines but also decreases in the utility of the goods, for example, due to obsolescence.

2. *Goodwill.* In financial accounting, goodwill is recorded when it is purchased in a business combination. Goodwill is the excess of the price paid over and above the fair market value of the net assets acquired, and it reflects the ability of the acquired firm to earn above-normal accounting earnings. Put another way, goodwill in a conceptual sense represents the present value of above-normal net future cash inflows to the firm due to unrecorded intangible factors.

3. *APB Opinion No. 21 (1971)*. The present value rule, or the discounted cash flow method, is an accepted valuation procedure in economics, finance, and actuarial science, and its relevance in management accounting and decision making is reasonably clear. In financial accounting, however, the uniform use of this technique and its recognition as a generally accepted accounting principle (GAAP) has been limited. It was not until the 1970s that this technique was applied uniformly to long-term receivables and payables by *Opinion No. 21*. Earlier, *Opinion No. 5* (1964) and subsequently *Opinion No. 7* (1966) called for the present valuation only with respect to long-term lease obligations. In all cases where the present value rule has been applied in accounting, future cash flows are contractually determined, either as a finanacial agreement or as an installment purchase.

The SEC had required the present valuation of receivables and payables that involve long-term contractual agreements when they are noninterest-bearing or reflect unrealistic interest rates which eventually led to APB *Opinion No. 21* (1971). Under APB *Opinion No. 21*, interest is reflected as an opportunity cost on the books of account whether or not it is received or paid as such. Such opportunity cost is also characterized as imputed interest. Prior to issuance of *Opinion No. 21*, form was given more weight than substance in accounting, and if a note had been noninterest-bearing, usually it would have been recorded at face value without any consideration of imputed interest.

According to *Opinion No. 21*, if the interest rate is either unstated or unreasonable or if the amount of the note is significantly different from the fair market value of the property in question or from the fair market value of the note, then interest has to be imputed. Should the fair market value of the note or the property be known, then that value is used to impute the interest. Otherwise, the rate to borrow on the part of the maker of the note represents the imputed interest rate, or opportunity cost.

In APB *Opinion No. 21*, the present valuation method is applied to long-term notes exchanged for property, goods, or services when they are noninterest-bearing or bearing unrealistic interest rates.

Present valuation is not applied to regular trade receivables and payables coming due within a one-year period or the normal operating cycle of the firm, as shown in Exhibit 4.3.

4. *Investment Return.* Accountants traditionally relied on methods that judge the profitability or return of investment alternatives based on traditional accounting measures. The problem with accounting numbers, however, is related to the fact that accounting earnings and accounting returns are based on book values, which reflect a series of more or less arbitrary choices of accounting methods. The danger of judging investment opportunities based on accounting measures is clear. Ideally, investment opportunities should be evaluated based on their present values of future expected cash flows using risk-adjusted market rates of return. Much of the controversy related to the present value rule or present valuation has been covered in the finance and economics literature.

If the present value rule were used in accounting to recognize economic income on invested funds, then all the problems associated with opportunity costs, interest rate changes, and inflation rate changes (expected and unexpected) would have to be

Exhibit 4.3
APB *Opinion No. 21*: "Interest on Receivables and Payables"

Present Valuation Applies to:

Long-term notes exchanged for property, goods, or services when they are noninterest-bearing, or bear unrealistic interest rates.

Amortization of the discount or premium using the effective interest approach.

Present Valuation Does Not Apply To:

Regular trade receivables or payables coming due within the one year period or normal operating cycle.

Downpayments or deposits on goods, services, or property.

Typical activities of banks.

Transactions between parent and subsidiary companies.

considered. Since cash flows may well be synergistic, stemming from a joint utilization of various productive assets, the cash flows of individual assets may not be separable. In such a case, simple value additivity may not hold, and the financial position of a firm could not be disaggregated into independent accounts. Therefore, *surrogates*, the most common of which is historical cost, are used in accounting in lieu of present value.

5. *Substitute Measures for Historical Cost.* Since economic value is based on discounted future cash flows, the value of conventional accounting information may well be limited for security analysis. The danger of using historical accounting measures to judge investment opportunities is clear. Ideally, investment opportunities should be evaluated based on their present values of expected cash flows using risk-adjusted market rates of return. Historical cost figures have long been used as a surrogate measure of discounted cash flows. However, in periods of significant and prolonged price changes, historical costs tend to become irrelevant for assessing economic performance and the current value of a firm. Other surrogates for historical cost are current replacement costs and exit values.

The essential attribute of *current replacement cost* is the use of current entry prices to measure an asset—that is, the amount of cash that would presumably be paid to acquire a similar asset to the one owned. In this model, historical cost is replaced by the current replacement cost. While the replacement cost is less objective, it is more relevant to a firm in a period of rapidly changing prices when assets are used rather than sold. Income in current replacement cost accounting reflects a matching of current expenses on the basis of current replacement cost against current revenues.

The application of replacement cost in financial reporting may furnish relevant information under particular conditions because such an income measure may approximate economic income. In a perfectly competitive market, current replacement cost income and economic income would equate. Under imperfect competition, current replacement cost income may or may not approximate economic income (Revsine, 1970, pp. 513–23).

Exit values or market values for nondistress resale reflect the ability of the firm to adapt to a changing environment and thus represent a conceptually correct measure of the opportunity costs of a firm. In particular, exit values are relevant to decisions of whether to continue the use of an asset, whether to stay in business, or whether to liquidate the firm as a whole.

Exit valuation, in contrast to the conventional accounting and the current replacement cost models, does not involve cost allocations. The reason is that exit valuation is not a cost method but rather a value method. A key deficiency of exit valuation is that income measures are narrowly defined and do not describe revenues and expenses directly.

6. *Lease Contracts.* Long-term leases that are in substance purchases of property are capitalized by the lessee at the lower of either the present value of the basic lease payments or the fair market value of the leased asset at the inception of the lease. Stated differently, the asset leased is not reflected at more than fair value. To obtain the present value of the lease payments, the lessee uses as the discount rate (opportunity cost) the lower of two rates: the lessee's incremental rate to borrow and the lessor's interest rate implicit in the lease, assuming the lessee is aware of the latter rate. The application of the lower of these two rates to the lease payments produces a higher present value. This makes it more likely that the lessee will have to reflect the lease as an asset under the provisions of FASB *Statement No. 13,* "Accounting for Leases" (1976), which governs lease accounting. Statement 13 asserts that lessees are required to reflect a lease as an asset if at least one of the following four criteria applies:

1. The lease transfers ownership of the property to the lessee
2. The lease contains a bargain purchase option
3. The lease term is equal to 75% or more of the estimated economic life of the leased property
4. The present value of the minimum lease payments (excluding executory costs) equals or exceeds 90% of the fair value of the leased property

For the lessor, the capitalization criteria are the same as for the lessee—that is, at least one of the foregoing four must be met—in addition to two other criteria:

1. Collectibility of the payments required from the lessee is reasonably predictable
2. No important uncertainties surround the amount of unreimbursable costs yet to be incurred by the lessor under the lease

7. *General Price-Level Adjustments.* The aim of general price-level accounting is to restate the unit of measurement to reflect common dollars, that is, dollars having the same purchasing power. In periods of rising prices, the buying power of the dollar will fall. This model, in contrast to conventional accounting, recognizes the fact that money value fluctuates with price-level changes. The dollar becomes inappropriate to use as a measurement unit in financial reports during periods of significant inflation.

The *constant-dollar model* constitutes an effort to deal with general inflation, but leaves unresolved the weaknesses inherent in the historical cost principle. In periods of significant price fluctuation, historical accounting information becomes irrelevant for decision making. Only by remote coincidence do the inflation-adjusted historical cost figures equal current values.

8. *Deprival Value.* Deprival value is a concept underlying the now-defunct inflation-accounting standard FASB *Statement No. 33,* "Financial Reporting and Changing Prices" (1979). Deprival value or "value to the business" is the "lower of (1) current cost or (2) recoverable amount, where recoverable amount is measured at the higher of net realizable value and net present value of future cash flows" (par. 99h). The concept assumes that a firm has been deprived of the use of an asset, and the question is how much the firm would need to be paid to be compensated for the lost asset. If management were to replace the asset in the normal course of business, its deprival value would be the current cost of the asset. Should the asset not be replaced in the normal operations of the firm, the deprival value would be the higher of the net realizable

value or the present value of discounted cash flows, the latter figure assuming the asset were used until worn out. Baxter (1975, p. 126) demonstrated the applicability of deprival value: "If a thief threatens to make off with one of your assets, but offers to refrain if you pay enough, what is the highest sum that he can prise [take] from you? Usually your ceiling will be replacement cost—i.e., this is . . . deprival value. But sometimes you will stick at a lower figure, because you do not deem the asset worth replacing; here the lower figure takes over as deprival value." Thus, deprival value is an opportunity cost (i.e., a foregone value).

There are six cases implicit in deprival valuation which are reflected below in Exhibit 4.4.

9. *Determining the Fair Market Value in Exchange of Goods for Securities*. In exchanges of nonmonetary items such as noncash assets given in exchange for capital stock, financial accounting uses the more verifiable fair market value to record the

Exhibit 4.4
Six Valuation Cases

Valuation cases	Presumed course of action and implication
(1) $PV^{(a)} > NRV > CC^{(b)}$	Replace to use; it may well be unlikely for NRV to exceed CC
(2) $CC > PV > NRV^{(c)}$	Use until the asset is worn out; do not replace it
(3) $CC > NRV > PV$	Sell; the firm, or its assets or asset, seems ready for liquidation
(4) $PV > CC > NRV$	Replace to use
(5) $NRV > CC > PV$	Replace to sell, which seems unrealistic
(6) $NRV > PV > CC$	Replace to sell, which seems unrealistic

(a) PV = Value in use
(b) CC = Current cost
(c) NRV = Net realizable value (current replacement cost or historical cost/constant dollar may replace CC in conformity with Statement No. 33).

transaction. In effect, two transactions can be imputed as the cash received from the issuance of capital stock at the fair market price, and as the cash being used in turn to purchase assets at their fair market price.

APPLICATION EXAMPLES OF THE OPPORTUNITY COST PRINCIPLE

Given the large number of decisions in which accounting information is used in conjunction with the opportunity cost principle, we present a number of examples where the opportunity cost is critical for determining the correct solution. Since it is the unique environment in which decisions are made that determines the final conclusion, a problem statement must be fully defined. It is this aspect of decision analysis which is important to recognize when applying simple decision rules.

Example 1

Given the case in which a firm produces superwidgets for sale in the market, with the following data assumed:

Variable Production Cost:	VC =	$32/unit
Fixed Production Cost:	FC =	$1,000/period
Market Price:	P_{sw} =	$60/unit
Production or Sales Volume:	X =	100 units/period
Profit:	=	$P_{sw} \cdot X - VC \cdot X - FC$
	=	(60) (100) − (32) (100) − 1,000
	=	$1,800/period

Assuming that the production is continuous and the production period is one month and that the owner has an offer to sell the firm for $210,000, the question is whether or not the offer should be accepted.

Considering this question purely as an investment decision, and ignoring certain technical questions, risk, and taxes, the answer depends on other investment opportunities for the money received. The rate of return on the apparent market value can be determined as:

$$\text{ROI} = \frac{(1800) \ (12)}{210,000} = 10.28\% \ \text{annually}$$

Given the case where the comparable market return is 12%, then the offer is too high. By not accepting the offer, the owner would incur an opportunity cost relative to the market of 1.72%. Rational behavior on the owner's part would *dictate a sale*. The question of why such an offer has been made, which would seem to be irrational on the buyer's part, is explained in Example 4.

Example 2

During a product review of the manufacturing process, it is found that an intermediate product could be sold as an ordinary widget. The following data are determined:

Widgets:

Variable Production Cost:	$VCw = \$12/\text{unit}$
Fixed Production Cost:	$FCw = \$400/\text{period}$
Market Price:	$Pw = \$15/\text{unit}$

Superwidgets:

Incremental Variable Cost:	$VCsw = \$20/\text{unit}$
Incremental Fixed Cost:	$FCsw = \$600/\text{period}$
Market Price:	$Psw = \$60/\text{unit}$

The question is raised whether the firm should purchase the widgets in the market rather than produce them. The answer to this question depends on different sets of assumptions with respect to the alternative use of the freed production capacity if the widgets are purchased:

a. Assumptions: The freed capacity cannot be channeled to any other use, and has no salvage value; additionally, fixed cost are eliminated by closing the facility.

Total Cost Approach

Cost of Producing: $VCw \cdot X + FCw = (12)(100) + 400$
                       $= \$1,600/\text{period or } \$16/\text{unit}$

Cost of Purchasing: $Pw \cdot X = (15)(100)$
                       $= \$1,500/\text{period or } \$15/\text{unit}$

Differential Cost Approach

Difference in cost $=$ Cost of Purchase $-$ Cost of Producing

$$= Pv \cdot X - VCw \cdot X - FCw$$

$$= (15)(100) - (12)(100) - 400$$

$$= \$100/\text{period}$$

$$\text{or } -\$1/\text{unit}$$

Thus, there is a \$1/unit cost differential in favor of purchasing. By producing the units, the firm incurs an opportunity cost of \$1/unit relative to the purchasing alternative. A rational decision would be to purchase the units and abandon the facilities.

b. Assumptions: The freed capacity cannot be employed in other uses, and the fixed costs remain the same regardless of which alternative is chosen.

Total Cost Approach

Cost of Producing: $VCw \cdot X + FCw = (12)(100) + 400$
                       $= \$1,600/\text{period or } \$16/\text{unit}$

Cost of Purchasing: $Pw \cdot X + FCw = (15)(100) + 400$
                       $= \$1,900/\text{period or } \$19/\text{unit}$

Differential Cost Approach

$$\begin{aligned}
\text{Difference in cost} &= \text{Cost of Purchase} - \text{Cost of Producing} \\
&= Pw \cdot X + FCw - VCw \cdot X - FCw \\
&= (Pw - VCw)\, X \\
&= (15 - 12)\,(100) \\
&= \$300/\text{period} \\
&\qquad \text{or } \$3/\text{unit}
\end{aligned}$$

There is a \$3/unit cost differential in favor of producing. Accordingly, the rational decision would be to produce the units.

c. Assumptions: The freed capacity can be leased (L) for \$600/period, and the fixed cost remains the same under both alternatives.

Total Cost Approach

Cost of Producing: $VCw \cdot X + FC = (12)\,(100) + 400$
$= \$1,600/\text{period}$

Cost of Purchasing: $Pw \cdot X + FC - L = (15)\,(100)$
$+400 - 600 = \$1,300/\text{period}$

Differential Cost Approach

$$\begin{aligned}
\text{Difference in cost} &= \text{Cost of Purchase} - \text{Cost of Producing} \\
&= Pw \cdot X + FC - L - VCw \cdot X - FC \\
&= (Pw - VCw)X - L \\
&= (15 - 12)\,100 - 600 \\
&= -\$300/\text{period} \\
&\qquad \text{or } -\$3/\text{unit}
\end{aligned}$$

There is a \$3/unit cost differential in favor of purchasing. By producing the units, the firm incurs an opportunity cost of \$3/unit relative to the purchasing alternative. The rational decision would be to purchase the units and lease the facilities.

d. Assumptions: The freed capacity can be sold for a price of $30,000, and the fixed costs are eliminated.

This analysis requires knowledge of the return that the firm can earn on the funds. Using the market interest rate of 12% as the opportunity cost of money, the periodic cash receipts of investing $30,000 in the market can be determined.

Given: Production Period   = 1 month
         Market Interest Rate   = 12% compounded monthly
         Periodic Cash Receipts (I) = (.01) (30,000) = $300/period

Total Cost Approach

Cost of Producing: $VCw \cdot X + FC = (12)(100) + 400$
                        $= \$1,600/period$

Cost of Purchasing: $Pw \cdot X - I = (15)(100) - 300$
                        $= \$1,200/period$

Differential Cost Approach

Difference in cost = Cost of Purchase − Cost of Producing

$$= Pw \cdot X - I - VCw \cdot X - FC$$

$$= (15)(100) - 300 - (12)(100) - 400$$

$$= -\$400/period$$

$$\text{or } -\$4/unit$$

There is a $4/unit cost differential in favor of purchasing. By producing the units, the firm incurs an opportunity cost of $4/unit relative to the purchasing alternative. The rational decision would be to purchase the units and to sell the facilities.

Example 3

During the product review meeting, it was also recognized that widget production could be increased to 200 units/period without changing the cost structure. The additional 100 units/period could be sold for $15/unit.

Since the firm produces joint products, only the incremental impact of changing the production volume of widgets is of concern to this decision.

Differential Approach

$$
\begin{aligned}
\text{Change in Benefits} &= \text{New Alternative} - \text{Old Alternative} \\
&= Pw \cdot 100 - VCw \cdot 100 \\
&= (15 - 12)\ 100 \\
&= \$300/\text{period} \\
&\quad\text{or } \$1.50/\text{unit}
\end{aligned}
$$

By not selecting the new alternative, the firm has an opportunity cost of $300/period or $1.50/unit (widgets) relative to the old alternative. A rational decision would be to implement the new alternative.

Example 4

The offer of $210,000 for the firm (Example 1) appeared to be excessive considering the existing use of the assets. If the offer is made, already recognizing the new alternative use of assets (Example 3), then the rate of return on the apparent market value would be:

$$
\text{ROI} = \frac{(1,800 + 300)\ 12}{210,000} = 12\% \text{ annually}
$$

In this case, the offer already considered the value of the assets in an alternative use. The owner would be indifferent between keeping and selling the firm. Given that the offer considered in Example 1 reflects the fourth case, then the rate of return on the apparent market value is:

$$\frac{[(1,800 \; + \; 400) \; (12)]}{210,000} \; = \; 12.5\% \; \text{annually}$$

The offer is too low. By accepting the offer, the owner would incur an opportunity cost of 0.57% in relation to the market. Rational behavior on the owner's part would *dictate not to sell.*

PART III

Opportunity Cost and Practical Problem Solving

Practical problem solving is a term that is difficult to define. The dictionary defines a "problem" as anything that requires a solution or as any matter that involves difficulties, doubt, or uncertainties. Similarly the interpretation of the term "practical" ranges from specific methods that are currently practiced to any procedure which assesses usefulness or which balances advantages with disadvantages. Thus, practical problem solving is closely associated with *rational* solution methods which are applied to specific problem situations. As long as problems are well defined and properly understood, it is possible to determine an optimal solution using mathematical procedures. However, as problems become more complex, interdependent, poorly understood, and dynamically changing, the application of mathematical methods to find optimal solutions becomes increasingly more difficult. Furthermore, as a specific problem solution affects more than one individual, the possibility exists that individuals do not agree on the optimality of a particular solution. Thus, practical problem solving introduces aspects that are not easily treated within the framework of rational solution methods unless specific simplifying assumptions are introduced. One particular set of assumptions used to solve economic problems is associated with the free market model.

Within the context of this book we associate *practical problem solving* with business-related problems faced by practitioners. These types of problems are usually multidimensional, interrelated, and dynamically changing, as well as affecting a variety of different individuals and society as a whole. Such *practical problems* differ from problems treated within theoretical models concerned with mathematical optimization procedures. We therefore distinguish between a practical domain and a theoretical domain of financial management. While the *theoretical domain* is concerned with model building and theory testing using positive and normative approaches, the *practical doman* involves the management of real business problems faced by practitioners. The main controversy in separating the two domains of financial management involves philosophical issues related to different beliefs and different views of the world.

Using a classification scheme which divides things into opposites, we can identify two extreme views of the world with a continuum between such as:

the Analytic View $\longleftrightarrow$ the Systemic View

The one extreme is the *analytic view,* which assumes that all things can be subdivided into small parts which themselves can be analyzed in isolation. As a result, the world can be viewed as a hierarchical structure of things, made up of parts, subparts, and atomistic elements. It is the task of researchers and philosophers to identify those parts and to discover their relationships and the mechanisms by which they interact. By structuring and grouping things in a particular order, it is possible to formulate analytic models that describe the structure and interactions of things in terms of particular hierarchical orders and specific cause-effect relationships. As in mechanical physics, equilibrium states exist in which offsetting forces balance, so that no changes occur whenever an equilibrium state is reached. It is the concern with equilibrium analysis that is addressed in the theoretical domain of financial management.

The other extreme is the *systemic view*, which assumes that the world can be represented by some suprasystem of interrelated and interdependent system components, which themselves represent systems that are composed of subsystems and components, all contributing specific attributes to the special characteristics of larger systems. Thus, within systems each subsystem and component contributes specific functions that are interrelated in a particular way as to determine the unique features of the larger system to be viewed as a whole. At each system level there exist interactions between the internal and the external environments. An example is the recognition of the interrelated dependencies between species in terms of food chains within ecological systems. Systems differentiate themselves from groups. Elements within a group possess common properties making them part of a group by some classification scheme, but member elements do not interact in any particular way.

The notion of *equilibrium* within a systemic view involves all aspects of internal and external environments within multidimensional interrelationships. All things are interrelated in some way, and disturbances in any particular subsystems will affect other larger and smaller system components. For example, the introduction of a particular chemical component into the environment will not only benefit the producers and users, but also affect other system components such as the food chain or the ozone layer. These effects will ultimately change a particular balance and in time alter the notion of benefits and practicality. Thus, within the systemic view the idea of a mechanical equilibrium state is replaced by the notion of natural balances.

For practical purposes both views contain useful applications. Particular problem situations may lie within the continuum between the two extreme positions. The *free market model*, derived within the analytic framework of rational and atomistic economic entities and associated with values outside of science, has become an ideal which is defended against new and perversive ideas. Seen as a guarantor of individual freedom, as a self-regulating mechanism to attain a natural equilibrium state, and as the cause for unprecedented economic welfare, the free market ideal has become the foundation of accepted social and political values. Although certain unfortunate side effects seem to be associated with this ideal, such as cyclical instability, poverty of some less fortunate, or the excessive exploitation of natural resources, these shortcomings are seen as being natural or caused by unwarranted interferences in the mechanism of free market pricing. It is the role of *government* to assure a free-market environment but not to interfere directly. The political assumption behind good government is rooted in the belief that free elections will guarantee government policies which reflect the will of electorates. Given the assumption that rational individuals know what is best and that government is responsive, able, and willing to implement appropriate policies, then the role of government becomes a matter of adhering to the *normative ideals* described by the free market model. However, several things may go wrong in a political process where the public decides on its desired goals which are then implemented by technicians in government. Besides the possibility that the public does not know enough about the complexities of interrelated social, political, and economic systems, there is the problem of a majority overriding the legitimate interests of minorities, and the possibility of government officials pursuing their own interests instead of those of the public. All these potential difficulties can be avoided by making appropriate assumptions. By treating only partial aspects of a more interrelated and complex reality and by disregarding undesired complications in an effort to attain simple, structured, and analytic models, one can attain any level of problem simplification. A justification for such *simplifying approaches* can be found in the long history of analytic model building and arguments established in science, as well as the implied usefulness of predicting specific observations or the ability of solving perceived practical problems.

To separate *financial management* into a practical and a theoretical domain requires not only a distinction between two aspects of financial problem solving, but also a clear understanding of different underlying concepts and principles that guide actions within the two domains. As a rough framework, we associate the theoretical domain with analytic model building using normative ideals and accepted scientific methods. In contrast, the practical domain is more closely related to a systemic view of organizations that pursue specific objectives through active management processes. While the goal of scientific methods is the discovery of scientific truth and the identification of natural laws that govern behavior, the goal of practitioners is associated with the management of complex, interrelated, and dynamically changing business conditions. Thus, in financial management, theoretical models attempt to explain the observed consequences of actions taken by practitioners. Instead, practitioners perform the required work to reach specific objectives and to cope with realistic, multidimensional, and dynamically changing business environments.

It is the close association of the practical domain with the theoretical domain, both defined within the analytic view of problem solving and scientific methods, which makes the *effort to separate* the two domains a difficult task. In finance, there is a close link between theoretical model building and practical problem solving by adopting an analogy between economic models and the mechanistic view of the world as promulgated by Newtonian physics during the eighteenth and nineteenth centuries. While most of the basic *mechanical assumptions* in physics have been upset by discoveries in the twentieth century, the ideals of classical economic models are still well accepted as the basis for economic decision making, at least in finance and accounting. For example, the belief in the existence of stable and natural equilibrium states that are determined by offsetting forces in terms of actions and reactions can be seen as the motivation to apply equilibrium models in economics also. Within the classical market model, equilibrium market prices are established by the offsetting forces of aggregate demand and aggregate supply. Once equilibrium has been reached, there is no incentive for change.

While *classical economic models* are concerned with a long-run equilibrium toward which a free market system will naturally evolve if left to free market forces, more recent market theories in finance apply equilibrium arguments to explain current prices in financial markets. By utilizing arguments of rational expectation, informational market efficiency, and present value based on discounting future expected cash flows, an individual can interpret observed capital market prices in terms of a continuous information market equilibrium. Market prices fluctuate in response to new information disseminated by the market. Also, if one accepts the idea of natural market equilibrium states for practical problem solving, decision making in finance becomes a matter of passively reacting to market-determined price information in an effort to optimize current wealth by following the market rule.

Within a *market equilibrium model,* opportunity cost becomes a rather specific concept: (1) As a criteria of equilibrium, all opportunity costs have been eliminated. In the long run this involves the optimal allocation of all resources and in the short run the optimal pricing of all resources. (2) As a criterion for decision making, opportunity cost is a measure of the degree of disequilibrium. It is the postulated optimization behavior of rational individuals who will eliminate such opportunity costs, thus providing the mechanism for attaining an equilibrium state. It is the concern with particular environmental structures which leads to specific decision and specific pricing models. Given a set of particular assumptions, equilibrium states can be defined by the Law of One Price, the absence of economic profits, or the nonexistence of opportunity costs. Equilibrium may involve arbitrage arguments, the value additivity principle, separation principles, or the present value rule. It is the set of necessary and sufficient assumptions which will fully define the problem statement, the model as well as the optimal solution.

This model-building approach follows the *principles of science* by which specific models are confronted by reality. As long as a model predicts observed experience, it is accepted as reflecting natural laws. The knowledge of natural laws makes the solving of practical problems a matter of properly specifying a problem and then applying the proper solution method. This type of practical problem solving is associated with *engineering-type problems* where natural laws determine fixed relationships among particular problem parts. It is the role of the theoretical domain in physics to discover such natural laws by using accepted scientific methods that involve model building and theory testing. Once such theories have been verified, they can be used by engineers in the practical domain to solve specific practical problems. With sufficient experience a practical problem solving procedure can be delegated and performed by computers.

Thus, the basic issue in separating a theoretical domain from a practical domain of financial management is related to some basic questions:

1. How closely do financial problems correspond to engineering-type problems?
2. How well are "natural laws" known to govern financial affairs?
3. How meaningful is the analogy between finance and mechanical models of physics?

Inasmuch as answers to these questions fall outside of the objective scientific realm, they can be addressed only in terms
of arguments that involve philosophical and methodological
issues. For example, by utilizing arguments involving economic
rationality and the opportunity cost principle, any practicing
rational individuals will adopt specific models and procedures
for practical problem solving *only* as long as they are useful
and profitable. Thus, models will be adopted by practitioners
only as long as they provide *profitable consequences.* Unless
otherwise requested by authorities or the "prudent man rule,"
models will be selected based on *practical usefulness.*

The static nature of long-run equilibrium models or the
analysis of comparative statics of microeconomic models
highlights the potential for practical difficulties when these
models are applied within the practical domain to solve practical problems within a multidimensional, interrelated, and
dynamically changing business environment. As normative or
positive scientific models, economic theories do have their place
within the theoretical domain, but they lack practical usefulness
in the practical domain. Contemplating the stock-market volatility in 1987 or 1988 may help us in this deliberation.

When addressing the *practical domain of financial management,* it becomes important to clearly understand the nature
of financial model building and the theoretical framework in
which opportunity cost has been defined. Given the evolutionary
change in the objectives and interpretations of economic models
over time, it is important to appreciate different underlying
philosophical and methodological positions as they relate to
specific economic and financial theories. While this potentially may lead to many discussions, arguments, and deliberations,
especially since deep-seated beliefs and controversial issues are
involved, we will keep the presentation as brief as possible.
Within this general idea, the following two chapters address
opportunity cost and descriptive interpretations of financial
management and opportunity cost and practical problem-solving
processes.

5

Opportunity Cost and Descriptive Interpretation of Financial Management

Descriptive interpretations of economic theories have been limited largely because of the complexities inherent in the real world. If one uses simple economic arguments, either in terms of general normative guidelines, for example, to discuss the role of government policies, or in terms of positive models, for example, to justify specific data analysis procedure, then a descriptive interpretation of economic models has been considered either axiomatic or unnecessary. Thus classical economic theory, concerned with the characteristics of a long-run equilibrium, is purely based on axioms defining rational behavior and assumptions specifying the structure of ideal competitive markets. These assumptions can be interpreted as the necessary and sufficient conditions required to describe the characteristics of a long-run competitive market equilibrium. While other possible scenarios exist, the underlying assumptions implied by the classical competitive market equilibrium model have been well integrated into an accepted value structure. If we accept the assumptions of specific models as reflections of "reality," then the reality itself becomes associated with the model. As a consequence, it is difficult to distinguish between the model and perceived reality.

Opportunity cost, for example, can be interpreted purely as a tautology, as a reflection of reality, or as an instrument to attain specific desired conclusions. It is an accepted fact that opportunity costs are difficult to determine unless defined within a specific frame of reference, such as a perfect long-run market equilibrium. As a consequence, the opportunity cost principle can be stated as an equilibrium criterion in terms of the Law of One Price, the absence of arbitrage opportunities, or the nonexistence of excess economic profits. While these arguments imply a large number of necessary and sufficient assumptions, any conclusions are based on the fundamental tautology: Rational individuals always optimize.

A general interpretation of such rational optimization behavior includes psychic values as well as dynamic and multidimensional problems, which are addressed by some unknown *judgmental processes.* In order to attain an unrestricted optimum, individuals must be free (unconstrained), must possess ideal cognitive abilities as well as complete knowledge, and must have access to all possible alternatives. These conditions are implied by perfect market assumptions and by mathematical optimization procedures that require a complete problem definition. The opportunity cost principle, in addition, requires that all possible alternatives and combinations are clearly specified and ranked by preferences. If we recognize the practical limitations of such complete problem specification, then any meaningful application to practical problem solving must introduce specific qualifications.

A long-run equilibrium analysis implies a specific solution approach in which market prices have properly adjusted and where equilibrium prices are determined by anonymous market forces and atomistic market participants, such that: Value = Price, for all market participants. A long-run equilibrium condition is fully described by the necessary and sufficient assumptions of rational behavior and the market structure. Within a long-run competitive, atomistic, free market equilibrium, all opportunity costs are eliminated for all market participants. Given atomistic economic entities with equal objectives, an equilibrium condition can be discussed in terms of average or marginal conditions since: Marginal Price = Average Price.

Both of these concepts have been extensively used in finance and accounting, and they justify the value additivity principle. For example, the long-run equilibrium value of a firm, financed by debt and equity, can be determined by

$$V_F = V_D + V_E$$

with
$$V_D = \sum_{1}^{n_B} P_B = n_B \cdot P_B$$

$$V_E = \sum_{1}^{n_S} P_S = n_S \cdot P_S$$

where

$$V_F = \text{market value of a firm}$$

$$V_D = \text{market value of the firm's debt}$$

$$V_E = \text{market value of the firm's equity}$$

$$P_S = \text{price of a share}$$

$$P_B = \text{price of a bond}$$

$$n_S = \text{number of shares outstanding}$$

$$n_B = \text{number of bonds outstanding}$$

Similarly an argument can be made to demonstrate that in equilibrium the total value of a firm (V_F) must be independent of any specific financing arrangements. As long as the markets are perfect and complete, it can be shown that

$$V_F = V_D + V_E = \text{constant}$$

This value independence proposition follows logically from the set of assumptions implied by a classical long-run market equilibrium, and it states that the total value must be equal to the sum of its parts. Similarly a long-run market equilibrium analysis implies separation principles such that consumption decisions, investment decisions, and financing decisions all can be treated in isolation.

The separation principle and the value independence proposition have led to two approaches to evaluate the *investment decisions* of a firm within the net present value method. The first approach utilizes the prices of claims against the firm in order to establish the component cost of different financing sources, which are then used to calculate an average weighted cost of capital, in terms of

$$K_a = \Sigma \, W_i \, K_j$$

where

K_a = average weighted cost of capital

W_i = specific component cost of financing such as debt or equity

K_j = weighting factor

The average weighted cost of capital is used as a measure of the average opportunity cost or financing cost to a specific firm. As long as investment projects are small and within a constant risk class, the expansion in scale of a firm can be evaluated within the NPV method.

The second approach assesses the risk-adjusted opportunity cost of an asset (investment project) directly by utilizing the concept of perfect substitutes and the Law of One Price. Since different financing arrangements do not alter the value of assets in perfect and complete markets, investment projects can be evaluated directly using the appropriate risk-adjusted opportunity cost and the NPV method. One particular method to assess the relevant risk-adjusted opportunity cost is given by the capital asset pricing model, where

$$R^* = R_F + [E(R_M) - R_F] \cdot \beta$$

with

$$R^* = \text{the risk-adjusted opportunity cost}$$
$$R_F = \text{the risk-free rate}$$
$$E(R_M) = \text{the expected market rate of return}$$
$$\beta = \text{a statistical measure of risk}$$

While in perfect markets and equilibrium, strict value additivity applies, it is the existence of market imperfections (transaction costs, taxes, imperfect information), synergism, and economies of scale which lead to potential windfall gains (losses) when larger investment projects are merged or consolidated within one firm. Thus, by increasing the complexity of decision problems and the environment in which decisions are made, it becomes necessary to consider the multidimensional characteristics of investment decisions including legal, tax, and strategic concerns. It is the full complexity of dynamically changing business environments that must be considered in practical decision making.

Utilizing the long-run equilibrium analysis within microeconomic models and comparative statics, it can be demonstrated that individual economic entities that are not yet in equilibrium can base their decisions on the *market rule*. Given market-determined, long-run equilibrium prices, a firm passively adjusts production volume and capacity decisions based on the market rule and the opportunity cost principle. In disequilibrium with respect to the long-run market equilibrium, a firm incurs an opportunity cost with respect to the market. Rationality dictates to eliminate such opportunity cost. A decision analysis can be based on an average (full) analysis or marginal (partial) analysis as long as the atomistic market assumptions and the value additively principle hold. Furthermore, since idealized long-run market equilibrium conditions imply separation principles and independence conditions, all production decisions, investment decisions, and financing decisions can be treated independently and in isolation. As a consequence of adopting a long-run equilibrium analysis, a rather specific view of decision making and practical problem solving has evolved.

Whenever the idealizing assumptions are relaxed, for example, by recognizing different tax rates for different individuals, then market equilibrium conditions in financial markets hold only at the margin. In this special case, value additivity holds strictly only for those marginal investors for which taxed and tax-exempt bonds are perfect substitutes. For all other market participants: Value $\neq$ Price.

Thus, by relaxing specific idealizing assumptions, we restrict the general applicability of a long-run equilibrium analysis. If we increasingly introduce more aspects of a complex reality into the analysis, then the validity of simple economic equilibrium arguments becomes questionable. It is, therefore, up to the discretion of model users whether to utilize these arguments for practical problem solving. Practical financial management, apart from the strictly atomistic market model, therefore becomes more unique, complex, and difficult than theoretical financial management.

MODEL BUILDING AND DESCRIPTIVE MODEL INTERPRETATIONS

Model building can be seen as a necessary means for dealing with an otherwise complex and confusing world. By utilizing abstractions, analogies, and metaphors, it is possible to address particular aspects of a problem and to communicate ideas, concepts, and observations. There are many different types of models, uses of models, and classifications of models, as well as many interpretations and philosophical positions with respect to what a model represents. For example, a language itself can be seen as a *model interpretation*. It is used to describe situations and relationships in words and thereby convey specific concepts and ideas. Thus, proper communication relies on a commonly accepted meaning associated with specific words. As new concepts are introduced, their interpretations have to be clearly defined. A language reflects commonly accepted ideals, which are based on the understanding of particular concepts during a particular period in time. The evolution of a language follows historical changes and, therefore, reflects an exercise in model interpretation.

Mathematics can be seen as a special language based on clear definitions that require quantitative measures and impeccable logic. Since mathematics is a language, all mathematical models can be expressed verbally. The advantage of mathematics is its precision and its ability to express complicated matters in relatively simple ways. Thus, modern theories such as quantum mechanics, wave mechanics, and general relativity theory all require mathematical formulations to communicate the content of these models. Another language is *sheet music,* which is used for the reproduction of a particular melody. To bring this music alive requires not only the technical skills of reading music, but also interpretation and imagination, besides an understanding of the time period in which the music was written. Thus, a connection exists between the mechanics of model building and the art of model interpretation.

The need to interpret models properly applies also to economic models. Given the wide variety of economic models, ranging from highly aggregated macromodels to particular micromodels and rather specific management models, utilizing various mathematical methods and a variety of mechanisms for model building provides a view of the wide latitude for model interpretation. Recognizing not only the evolutionary change of the environment from the time in which classical economic models were originally formulated, but also the variety of different views of the world and the changes of knowledge over time gives a sense of the wide range of possible *descriptions* implied by economic models. By selecting specific interpretations and by utilizing methodologies applied in natural sciences, economic models have become arguments that attempt to discover scientific truth. *Scientific methods,* however, require clear definitions, precise measurements, and objective criteria for model validation, which introduces new challenges to the interpretation of traditional economic models. This is especially of concern when normative economic models and the subjective opportunity cost concept are interpreted in terms of objectively measurable quantities, which are then used to explain observed economic behavior or to prescribe rational decision rules.

AN HISTORICAL INTERPRETATION OF ECONOMIC MODELS

Realizing the potential for confusion when economic models are interpreted in different descriptive ways, we review first some of the basic concepts of economic model building in general and scientific model building in particular. Given the inherent controversy with such an attempt and the variety of different methodological and philosophical positions, we will keep the discussion to a bare minimum. Since philosophical views do not evolve sequentially, we will also refrain from any historical chronology.

Classical economic theory as developed by Adam Smith or David Ricardo can be interpreted as a *normative model* that introduces the concept of free markets as an ideal based on private property rights and individual freedom as discussed by Locke or Hume. As a normative ideal, the free market concept represents an alternative to feudalism, mercantilism, and centrally controlled economic systems, providing the basis for currently accepted social and political values. By utilizing an analogy with classical mechanical physics as introduced by Newton and the analytic approach to model building which had been set forth by Aristotle, we can see human behavior as being directed by natural forces that guide economic systems passively into a stable, self-regulating, long-run equilibrium. This view provides the basis for many philosophical arguments, a justification to search for evidence of such natural forces, as well as attempts to predict the natural evolution of human organizations over time.

The *scientific approach* for discovering the truth about the mechanical universe is based on reasoning, mathematical logic, and empirical validation as popularized by Newton. The scientific approach requires the adherence to strict rules in order to eliminate subjective values from the analysis and to enable the replication of research findings by others. The goal of the scientific method is the discovery of natural laws. As such, normative concerns are usually not addressed. For example, the question "should the earth rotate around the sun" has no meaning today, even though it was central to discussions in the 16th and 17th centuries, when initiated by Galileo. The scientific approach represents a logical procedure for discovering the nature of things, which differs profoundly from conditions where permissible questions and acceptable answers are determined by authoritative institutions representing specific ideologies, enforcing particular doctrines, or upholding special dogmatic interests. It is the impressive success of scientific methods in natural sciences which has led to the many technical achievements that are shaping our daily lives and which has reinforced the belief in science as a way to find answers to all types of questions.

Applying the scientific approach to interpret classical normative economic theories has led to a variety of methodological and philosophical arguments. It is the acceptance of an analogy between natural sciences and social sciences which has created a large number of scientific-type studies also in finance, economics and accounting. In particular, it is the analogy with mechanical physics and scientific methodologies prevalent in the nineteenth century which has provided the basis for many of the scientific interpretations of normative classical economic models. To appreciate different descriptive interpretations of financial management, it is therefore important to recognize the evolution of scientific thought over time. If we adhere to specific interpretations of financial theories, then much of the complex reality can be ignored. While this has advantages in the theoretical domain, practitioners faced with practical problem solving do not have the option to ignore undesirable complications.

During the long *history of scientific thought*, various methodological positions evolved with respect to model building and theory testing. The possiblility of classifying models by different classification schemes leads to a multitude of model types reflecting different model uses, different model structures, and different definitions of what a model actually represents. Without addressing any of these details, we distinguish among the following components: *assumptions, models, and consequences.* Depending on specific methodological positions, we identify characteristics that are assigned to these components:

Assumptions	Models	Consequences	Methodological Positions
true	true	true	Synthetic Apriorism
validate	validate	true	Empiricism
validate	validate	validate	Realism
instrument	validate	true	Positivism (Instrumentalism)
instrument	instrument	validate	Critical Rationalism

Synthetic apriorism (Immanuel Kant) holds that models represent solely a system of logical deduction from a series of synthetic assumptions (axioms) of unquestionable truth. Thus, specific assumptions on which such models are based are not open to empirical verification or a general appeal to objective experience. Thus, a model and its conclusions must be true if logically derived from a true set of assumptions. By contrast, the methodological positions of *empiricism* and *realism* require the validation or falsification of different components. The position of *positive economics,* as formulated by Milton Friedman, considers the assumptions on which a model rests, purely as instruments introduced only to derive the model in the first place. The model itself is validated by its ability to predict the behavior of any endogenous variable treated by the model. This methodological position has led to the expansion of pure data analysis on the grounds that the model itself is validated by its ability to "explain" (predict) the data. A more reserved position is expressed by *critical rationalism*, which holds that the goal of research should be to falsify existing theories. As long as falsification does not occur, any theory should be considered as "not yet falsified" (Popper, 1959). Any claim of a theory to hold timeless truth must be rejected. Interpreting economic models by their descriptive and normative implications makes the assumptions, the model, and the consequences instruments to attain desired outcomes. That is why classical economic theories are not scientific models.

The derivation of specific economic models based on mathematical procedures, requires assumptions that are specified by the mathematical procedure itself. Thus, the use of a particular *mathematical method,* such as functional analysis, topology, set theory, and statistics will ultimately specify the necessary and sufficient assumptions that define the final model. This is reflected, for example, in mathematical definitions that specify rational behavior (theory of rational choice) or that determine the definitions of a perfect competitive market or that establish criteria of an equilibrium condition. Interpreting economic models by their normative implications makes mathematical presentations of classical economic models pure instruments to attain desired results. While the building of a mathematical model must follow precise rules and logical procedures, its acceptance as a useful model involves such things as:

Predictive accuracy

Descriptive reality

Prescriptive ease

Practical benefits

Argumentative persuasiveness

Logical consistency

Adherence to ''accepted'' views and values

Economic model building is, therefore, difficult to separate from normative implications, political reality, subjective judgments, and existing ideologies. The belief that mathematics is value-free can be seen as one reason why scientific interpretations of economic models in terms of positive economics has become a dominant view, the use of mathematical logic an accepted procedure, and the validation of assumptions as instruments an unnecessary task. This ignores, however, the observation that mathematics is just a different type of language which is based on specific axioms assumed to be true (synthetic apriorism).

DESCRIPTIVE MODELS AND PRACTICAL PROBLEM SOLVING

The attempt to interpret economic models, with respect to their descriptive reality or to their usefulness to practical problem solving, introduces a variety of complications. A *descriptive model* depends on the specific purpose for which the model has been designed. For example, a map to guide an individual from point A to point B may require only a sketch of a few main streets. The practical usefulness of this descriptive model can only be evaluated in retrospect by the success of reaching the destination without a lot of complications. Therefore, criteria to judge the performance of a descriptive model depend on the particular use and the particular user. This applies especially to practical problem solving. For example, a model designed to increase understanding of an otherwise complex and confusing situation can be judged only by its effectiveness to actually increase understanding. This, however, can be evaluated only in retrospect, when the acceptance of an initial model gives rise to the development of a better solution. To discover a better solution requires, however, a better understanding and with that the possibility to create a better model. The development of understanding is therefore associated with a *learning process*.

With respect to practical problem solving, the effectiveness of a particular model can also be evaluated only in retrospect. The problem can be solved after developing an initial understanding of a particular problem situation with the help of a particular model. However, only after a better understanding of the problem has evolved is it possible to find a better solution. To discover a better solution requires, however, a better model. Trying to discover a better solution involves an *experimental process* that allows for measures of success and failure. Thus, practical problem solving involves learning processes and experimental processes, unless the problem is already known. In the specific case where a problem is known and well understood, the solution is attainable by solving a particular known model. This type of practical problem solving is applied in engineering where a model properly reflects a known reality. In this special case there is no need to discover better solutions or better models.

By adopting the view that free market forces guarantee optimality, any economic and *financial problem solving* requires just the passive adjustment to given long-run market equilibrium prices by following the market rule. Thus practical problem solving implies only the proper application of specific equations and mathematical optimization rules. This type of problem analysis is implied by microeconomic models as introduced by Alfred Marshall in terms of comparative statics and the marginal analysis. Given long-run equilibrium prices, individuals adjust *passively* to attain optimality. This model does not allow for experimental learning processes since the environment is fully determined and known to all. As such, the model is deeply rooted in the deterministic-mechanical-analytic view of the universe. Given the assumptions of the role of money seen purely as a means for transacting market exchanges, financial management has no part in practical economic problem solving. This is reflected in the view that "money does not matter."

As an argument for the self-regulating forces in an economic macrosystem, the opportunity cost principle is used in conjunction with deterministic models. Given that short-term conditions move individual market prices away from a long-run equilibrium, excess economic profit opportunities are created, which will be exploited by rational entrepreneurs. The opportunity cost principle will bring markets back into a long-run equilibrium. To eliminate the market disequilibrium, firms will increase production, investors will supply additional resources, and consumers will limit consumption. It is this *self-regulating price mechanism* which will bring economic systems back into a long-run equilibrium, as long as it is not prevented by unwarranted interferences of governments. All that is required is that rational individuals know opportunity costs created by market disequilibrium conditions. While theoretically convincing, the argument is based on a large number of idealizing assumptions that unfortunately are not descriptive of a more complex reality.

PRACTICAL PROBLEM SOLVING AS
AN EXPERIMENTAL PROCESS

Practical problem solving is related to the success of attaining a specific goal. For example, theories and models in finance are accepted by practitioners because of their implied ability to make money. Any concern with philosophical positions, model interpretations, or methodological implications is unimportant as long as the model works. Within this framework of *pragmatism,* theories and models are tested by actual realization attempts. This presents an experimental approach which may lead to success and fortune or to unexpected failure. Thus, practical models are validated based on experimental experience. Researchers may actively participate in this learning process and discover new *problem-solving processes.* Experimental methods are of particular interest when problems are novel, complex, interrelated, multidimensional, and poorly understood. As such, practical problem solving itself can be seen as an experimental process used to develop a better understanding of particular problem situations.

By adopting a systemic view of the world, practitioners find that most practical problems are associated with dynamically changing environmental conditions, so that the idea of a long-run stable equilibrium is not useful. Furthermore, the assumed certainty and deterministic view implied by theoretical models is only of limited usefulness to practitioners. Thus, the theoretical domain of financial management, by utilizing specific analytic simplifications and the concept of mechanical equilibrium conditions, exists largely independent of the practical domain. This fact is recognized not only by different problem situations treated within the practical domain, but also by the recognition that practical financial management problems cannot be solved in the same fashion as engineering-type problems. While this observation is dependent on particular value systems and views of reality, it highlights the need to separate the practical domain from the theoretical domain of financial management.

THE CHANGING CONCEPTS OF FINANCIAL MANAGEMENT

The idea of financial management has been changing all along, largely in response to an increasingly more complex environment, specific historical events, and different perceptions of money, as well as different models and theories pertaining to the management of economic systems. In classical economic models, the importance of financial management is limited. Based on barter and real economic activities, classical theories considered money purely as a medium of exchange. The value of money itself is based on its commodity value. This framework is associated with the *gold standard*, gold coins, and early banking institutions. While praised as a self-regulating mechanism, the gold standard was associated with frequent bank failures and panics. Though started in England in 1816, the gold standard era is more appropriately applied to the period 1880-1914 when most countries had adopted a rule which made paper money freely exchangeable for gold. The period after World War I saw drastic changes and the development of pure credit money. The value of *credit money* is not related to a commodity freely traded, but is managed by monetary authorities. As such, the idea of self-regulating economic systems was replaced by the need to properly manage the money supply and to maintain independent central banks to stabilize the banking industry. The varied experiences after World War I led to different international agreements and different theories with respect to the need to manage economic macrosystems.

While the role of financial management in economic macrosystems is still debated, financial management is more readily associated with the management of an economic microsystem. By utilizing the framework of rational choice and perfect competitive financial markets in equilibrium, the opportunity cost principle leads to particular *optimization rules*. A rational financial manager will or should follow the market rule so that in optimality the marginal productivity of capital is equal to the marginal cost of capital, or: MPC = MCC. Thus, within the theoretical domain, the *role of financial management* is clearly defined. To optimize involves the ranking of alternatives by the marginal productivity (internal rate of return) and a comparison with the market cost of capital. As a decision rule, this involves a number of important, necessary, and sufficient assumptions, besides the need to properly determine future expected cash flows. As an equilibrium criterion of a perfectly competitive long-run market equilibrium, this rule follows accepted methods of classical economic model building. As a practical management tool, it implies that the required information is available as well as that the underlying theoretical model is reflective of reality. As such, this optimality criterion involves specific philosophical positions and particular beliefs.

While it is possible to explicitly introduce risk and uncertainty into this decision rule or equilibrium criteria, the need for additional relevant information increases substantially. More recent financial market equilibrium models have introduced specific measures of risk and uncertainty into the analysis of observed financial market prices, based on statistical models and time series analysis, but the basic rule is still founded on the opportunity cost principle. Investment projects should be accepted as long as the risk-adjusted present value is larger or equal to the market value. Thus, the classical optimization based on following passively the market rule has not been changed.

To take a different perspective of financial management when viewed within the practical domain, we first review some of the basic controversies in the theories of managing economic macrosystems. This highlights the changing role of financial management in general and the function of financial markets specifically. In chapter 6, we will return to issues of financial management as applied to practical financial problem solving.

THEORIES OF MACROECONOMIC MANAGEMENT

Outstanding among the theories of how to manage economic macrosystems is the dispute between Keynesians and modern monetarists. After the stock market crash in 1929 and the resulting worldwide recession, Keynes (1936) challenged the classicial economic theory by suggesting that direct government intervention in terms of government work programs, fiscal policies, and deficit spending could prevent economic cycles and bring an economy out of a recession. As a consequence, the role of government increased drastically, which then led to moves to limit government in the 1980s. Milton Friedman as a founder of modern monetarism, on the other hand, argued that government intervention is destabilizing and that a stable money growth rate should be maintained. The Federal Reserve implemented a *monetary experiment*, which started in 1979 and ended in 1982, with questionable results. Recognizing the rather turbulent history of money and the changing theories pertaining to financial management, we review some of the basic issues related to financial models within the theoretical domain. In particular, we utilize a *descriptive approach* by emphasizing the nature and foundation of theoretical arguments. This approach distinguishes itself from scientific model interpretations which emphasize predictive precision in lieu of descriptive accuracy. Aspects of practical applications of such models within the practical domain of financial management are discussed in chapter 6.

The Classical Model

The classical macroeconomic model is based on the following scenario:

An economic system is subdivided into two mutually exclusive sectors, production and consumption. While the production sector is composed of atomistic firms that produce all goods and services, the consumption sector is composed of all the individuals who consume all the output, own all the resources, and hold all financial claims. Exchange occurs in perfect competitive markets represented by commodity markets, resource markets, and financial markets. Individuals are rational optimizers and only concerned with market exchange values.

Since everything is assumed to be perfect, the system will attain a *full employment equilibrium* at least in the long run. Any disturbances will be reflected in price changes, which automatically restore equilibrium by eliminating apparent opportunity costs. While this simple analytic model is based on many unrealistic assumptions and many simplifications, it provides the basis for many arguments which are summarized by the free market ideal.

The classical free market long-run equilibrium can be described by the following postulates:

1. "Supply creates its own demand." This postulate guarantees full employment of all resources as long as they are offered to the market. Any unemployment is voluntary or temporary. As long as market prices adjust freely to aggregate demand and supply conditions, the economic system will maintain a full employment equilibrium. This idea is referred to as Say's Law (Jean Baptiste Say).

2. "Money does not matter." This postulate has various interpretations and is summarized by the quantity theory of money. Within a modern interpretation, it states that any money supply that is not held by individuals will be spent and therefore affect the general price level. Since economic activity is related to real and not nominal values, money does not matter for making economic decisions. This implies that rational individuals will not suffer from money illusions and that all profitable projects will be financed. Rational individuals consider the purchasing power of money instead of the nominal amount of money they hold. This is especially so in an environment where money is associated with credit money, instead of commodity money.

3. Interest Rate Mechanism. If we separate the financial market from all other markets and treat it as a partial equilibrium, then interest rates are determined by an equilibrium between the aggregate demand and aggregate supply of loanable funds. Equilibrium is guaranteed through the flexible pricing mechanism in all markets. It should be remembered that the present value theory came about in the early 1900s, and it was more formally accepted as a method to determine equilibrium prices of capital assets in the 1930s (Irving Fisher, 1930).

The Keynesian Model

The classical free-market model evolved during the ninteenth century, and it provides many normative arguments and many scientific explanations for a vast number of observed phenomena. Its basic postulates are still the basis for many arguments and policy decisions that call for limited government interference and laissez-faire policies. While its conclusions and basic assumptions have been challenged by many, including Thomas Malthus and Karl Marx, it was John Maynard Keynes who in 1936 introduced a different approach to analyze an *underemployment equilibrium* of macroeconomic systems.

The classical economic model essentially eliminates the government sector from the analysis and treats an international equilibrium in isolation, following the tradition of analytic simplifications and partial equilibrium analysis. By contrast, Keynes made the government and the international sector part of the economic analysis. By addressing the consequences of the Great Depression in the 1930s, Keynes concluded that only government actions could affect an underemployment equilibrium and bring an economic system back to full employment. Thus, Keynes challenged the fundamental assumptions of classical economic theory by introducing the following postulates:

1. "Demand Creates Supply." This postulate makes it possible for economic systems to face equilibrium conditions with underemployment at least in the short run. Keynes argues that the price mechanism is not flexible enough, at least on the down side, to assure full employment. The existence of fixed capital resources and contractual agreements provides an incentive to reduce output to meet existing demand, instead of reducing prices to maintain full employment.

2. "Money Does Matter." This postulate recognizes money as an asset and recognizes a speculative demand for money. When security prices are expected to fall, it is rational to hold money balances (hoarding), which reduces the money supply available and which in turn reduces capital asset prices. This mechanism affects real economic activities and makes monetary control of the money supply ineffective. To get

out of this dilemma requires active fiscal government policies in order to restore full employment. The self-regulating forces of the classical model work to slow and create a lot of suffering which can be avoided.

3. Interest Rate Mechanism. Interest rates are determined by the aggregate demand and supply of money. Through the speculative demand for money, interest rates may not respond to monetary expansion and the demand for money in the real economy, thereby jeopardizing the self-regulating mechanism of classical economic theory.

The Keynesian theory led to the belief in a much larger role of government policies to stabilize and manage the economic affairs of a macroeconomic system. In time, large-scale computer simulation models evolved which attempt to represent structural and behavioral characteristics associated with specific sectors of an economic system as well as interrelationships among different sectors. While these representations of reality provide a basis for policy analysis, their success has been limited, largely because of the mechanical nature of these models. The realization that human system behavior is more complex and interdependent, plus less mechanical, has led to the theories that recognize adaptive and anticipating behavior. Because of its failure to provide solutions to continuous inflationary price changes during the 1970s, the Keynesian approach became suspect, and it was replaced by modern monetarism.

The Modern Monetarism

By attempting to predict the behavior of aggregrate income through various measures of the money supply, Milton Friedman and others revived the classical quantity theory of money. Friedman rejected the simplistic *cause-effect* chains of reasoning used by the Keynesian approach. By arguing that the behavioral relationships in human systems are far too complex to be modeled and that government policies may be the cause of instabilities and prolonged periods of booms and busts, modern monetarism revived the argument that the private economic sector is self-regulating and tends toward a long-run equilibrium if only left alone. Thus, the classical ideals of free markets and laissez-faire policies became important again. Believing that supply is the driving force of economic activity, tax reform was introduced in 1986 under the banner of *supply-side economics.* While it is possible to argue that such policy decisions follow a Keynesian analysis, it is the belief in a limited role of government to manage economic affairs that is the essence of modern monetarism.

Recognizing the argumentative and normative nature of economic theories, it is the underlying view of human system behavior that underlies model building and arguments. By acknowledging the complexities and multitudes of interrelationships that exist in economic systems, besides the effects of political and social interdependencies, modern monetarism analyzes a macroeconomic system as a *systemic whole,* without specific statements about the inner workings. The relationship between money and income is seen as determined by a complex but relatively stable *transmission process.* An overall equilibrium in the economic system can be discussed within a portfolio-balancing approach in which money is considered a particular type of asset. In equilibrium, the marginal risk-adjusted returns of all assets, including the imputed yields on consumer goods and durable commodities, must be equal so that no unexploited opportunity costs exist. Any money supply in excess of the public's willingness to hold will result in spending activities until all prices are adjusted and a new equilibrium is reached. In equilibrium, any excess money supply or demand is eliminated. Thus, inflationary price changes are a monetary phenomenon and should be treated as such. The adjustments in the real economy follow the postulates of the classical free-market model. Any shortages in the money supply will lead to downward price movements until a new equilibrium is reached. Thus, it is the classical belief in the pricing mechanism of free markets that guides modern monetarism.

A SYSTEMIC VIEW OF ECONOMIC MACROSYSTEMS

Including the government sector and the foreign sector into the equilibrium analysis provides arguments which call for balanced government budgets and balanced foreign trade relations. A stable equilibrium can be reached only when all sectors are in equilibrium. However, as long as deficits are financed by the foreign sector willing to hold financial claims denominated in dollars, there is no real need for change and unpopular political decisions. The free-market forces will work in time. Thus, it is the belief in classical economic models and the self-regulating mechanism of free markets that will guarantee a long-run equilibrium. Any isolated signs of potential instabilities, such as the stock market crash of 1987, the international debt crisis, or the prolonged bank crisis of savings and loans institutions, are lack and seen as temporary phenomena on the way to a stable long-run equilibrium. What is required is deregulation, free markets, and the reduction of government interference.

What this position and the call for more freedom from government interference lack is a more descriptive interpretation of economic models. By relying on mechanistic models and scientific methods to analyze past experiences, we neglect the *experimental nature* of human system evolution. Current environmental conditions and economic circumstances are unique and different from conditions in the past, especially from conditions prevailing in the 1800s or from the conditions during the 1930s, 1940s, and 1950s. It is the long-standing belief in the mechanistic, analytic, deterministic, and atomistic nature of the world which retains the faith in classical economic models. Scientific truth can only be found in measurable experiences of the past. By believing in natural forces and a stable mechanical equilibrium, classical models ignore the effects of unprecedented population growth, technological change, or the limitations of life-supporting natural resources, among many other aspects of more complex human organizations.

By accepting the notion of a *systemic approach* as an extreme opposite to the analytic approach, the classical economic models become suspect by addressing only isolated aspects of human organizational behavior. As an integral part of larger ecological systems and the natural environment, human organizations can be viewed in terms of interrelationships with their internal and external environments. Instead of a mechanical equilibrium among offsetting forces, cause-effect relationships, and mechanisms that control the behavior of individuals, an *"organizational equilibrium"* can be viewed in terms of a balance among the multitude of interrelated systems, subsystems, and supra-systems within a multidimensional environment. Within a systemic view, any solution to a particular problem is interrelated with other system components. Problems do not exist in isolation, and particular solutions interact with environmental conditions in mysterious and unknown ways. An organizational balance may be disturbed, thereby creating new situations through adaptive behavior. There is no optimum to be reached.

Classical economic models emphasize the importance of government in terms of guaranteeing a competitive and free-market environment in order to attain a stable long-run equilibrium by self-regulating market forces. Keynesian economics recognizes the importance of government control to maintain stability. Such a *control aspect* is especially important after the introduction of credit money, the quantity of which is controlled by monetary policies. As such, the political impact on economic systems behavior has been recognized. The linkage among social, cultural, and religious affiliations on political processes, the impact of the legal system, or the lobbying effects of special interest groups on government policies all highlight the complex interrelationships within human organization systems. It is the concern with specific *control processes,* which is important for maintaining a balance between internal and external environmental conditions, that is of interest in a systemic view.

A multidimensional and dynamic systemic view of human organizational evolution provides a more descriptive model of financial management procedures. The question of how to manage macroeconomic affairs can only be addressed by considering the objectives, the environmental conditions, as well as their anticipated consequences. While such a complex view of organizational management and control of human systems lacks the simplicity of simple analytic arguments, it does introduce some interesting applications of the opportunity cost principle.

THE OPPORTUNITY COST PRINCIPLE
IN A SYSTEMIC VIEW

By defining opportunity cost in terms of objectively measurable quantities with respect to a long-run market equilibrium, the opportunity cost principle has become a criterion for specifying market equilibrium conditions. By assuming homogeneous atomistic market participants concerned only with market values that are determined in perfect competitive markets, a market equilibrium can be characterized by:

The Law of One Price

The absence of arbitrage opportunities

The nonexistence of excess profits

The elimination of all opportunity costs

These mechanical equilibrium conditions imply, among other conditions, value additivity, value equal to price, profit or wealth optimization, separation principles, independence propositions, and the equality of marginal and average values.

In such an idealized world, individual economic agents optimize by passively applying the market rule. The equilibrium conditions of a firm can be stated, therefore, in terms of passive profit or wealth optimization rules. In the long run, all resources will be optimally allocated and efficiently used by minimizing all explicit costs and by eliminating all implicit and opportunity costs. The underlying motive or force to reach such an equilibrium is the profit motive an well as the ability to freely exploit all opportunities. The process by which such an equilibrium state is reached can be stated in terms of the opportunity cost principle as: Eliminate *all* opportunity costs. This defines opportunity cost as being associated with any nonoptimal condition. It is the role of organizational management to reduce or to eliminate all opportunity costs.

This more general interpretation of the opportunity cost principle includes a variety of aspects. Firms should or will, therefore, develop new products, new production methods, new marketing strategies, and new organizational structures as soon as opportunity costs are realized by not changing, not developing new ideas, or not adapting to new environmental conditions. As such, it is the opportunity cost principle that guides organizational behavior. However, by pursuing their self-interest, individuals may utilize all kinds of methods to retain *competitive advantages* by eliminating competition and monopolizing markets. By giving up monopolistic advantages, those individuals in the position to monopolize incur an opportunity cost. Thus, the opportunity cost principle can also explain why individuals may try to eliminate or manipulate the conditions that specify an ideal free market environment.

Market manipulation may take a variety of forms, which range from the outright elimination of free markets to the prohibition of particular actions. As a normative ideal, the free market concept requires the government to assure an environment of free markets as specified by the requirements of classical market models. However, particular individuals or industries may find it beneficial to be protected from competitive market forces, through protective barriers or government subsidies. As a consequence, it is difficult to separate the political, economic, and social aspects within human organizations. As a normative ideal, the classical free market model has provided many arguments that demonstrate the benefits of individual freedom, of free trade, and of the right of individuals to pursue their own happiness. Within the systemic view of human organizations, these human rights are not questioned; only the importance of complex systemic interdependencies among participating system components is recognized.

The classical free market ideal provides simple arguments that demonstrate the benefits of free trade. On the other hand, it provides arguments that demonstrate negative impacts. As an argument, the model provides a basis for many studies in the theoretical domain of financial management, but as a practical management tool, there are difficulties when it is applied in the practical domain of financial management. Not only is reality more complex, interrelated, and dynamically changing, but the required information to optimize is usually not available. Instead of applying passive market optimization rules, individuals pursue *active strategies* to minimize their own opportunity costs. This, in the extreme, will lead to incentives to actively manipulate the political process by which governments control economic activities through monetary and fiscal policies. It also leads to active management procedures to develop new products, new procedures, and new organizational structures in an effort to gain competitive advantages. There is also the threat of political change, boycotts, hostile take-overs and leveraged buy-outs, that has created an environment in which practical financial management must consider specific strategies to counter such threats. All this can be seen as a manifestation that free market forces are at work or as an argument to more actively manage the financial affairs of organizational systems. While acknowledging that the process of change is continuously working, we discuss the role of financial management in the practical domain in the following chapter.

6

Opportunity Cost and Practical Problem Solving in Finance

Any formal definition of financial management is theory-based and is therefore dependent on the particular model in which the term is used. As such, financial management can refer to the acquisition of capital or assets; the issuing, trading, or extinguishing of financial contracts; the raising of money; the creation of value; the allocation and use of scarce resources; the management of cash flow; the optimization of financial positions; as well as any combination of the above.

Furthermore, financial management can relate to the financial affairs of individuals, business organizations, and government agencies, as well as macroeconomic systems and international monetary relations. In general, since all economic activities are associated with costs and benefits, they are affecting the financial position of an economic entity. Thus, financial management involves the fall range of economic activities.

Within the *accounting model,* the concept of financial management refers to the management of specific accounts associated with the income statement and the balance sheet. Inasmuch as economic activities are reflected in accounting statements, it is the role of financial management to find the proper structure of accounts and balance of accounting ratios with the goal of guaranteeing financial success. By relating the accounting model to the *market model,* financial management becomes associated with the goal to optimize market values. It is, therefore, the task of financial management to employ optimal asset and capital structures, as well as to assure the efficient use and optimal allocation of scarce economic resources. The concept of a long-run market equilibrium provides a framework to measure opportunity costs and criteria to optimize market value. While the financial accounting model is based on generally accepted accounting principles (GAAP), cost accounting models and managerial accounting models are designed to provide *relevant* information for economic decisions. By viewing the accounting model as a method to accumulate financial information based on transaction data, financial management becomes more appropriately associated with general management functions such as the planning, organizing, staffing, directing, and controlling of business affairs.

Within a *management model,* the function of financial management is dependent on specific organizational arrangements. Thus, financial management is concerned with the financial affairs of an organization related to the treasury function and the controllership function. The specific organizational philosophy as well as the size of an organization will define the specific tasks associated with each function. Within a *decision-making model,* financial management utilizes all necessary and relevant information to determine an optimal solution to any particular economic problem situation. Such relevant information will include accounting data and market data as well as information associated with the internal and external environments affecting a specific problem statement. Within the *atomistic market equilibrium model,* individual problem situations can be treated in isolation and different aspects separated with the goal of determining the optimal market value. Financial problem solving becomes increasingly more complex by relaxing the strict classical assumptions that define complete rationality as well as perfect, complete, competitive, and atomistic markets. Instead of searching for optimal solutions to well-specified problem statements, financial management becomes more readily identified with processes and strategies aimed at achieving specific objectives. The *strategic management model* addresses more complex, interrelated, multidimensional, and dynamically changing environments, so that financial management reflects specific strategic plans and management control procedures. Depending on circumstances that affect a particular economic problem situation, practical financial management must recognize the special conditions that determine a specific and unique problem situation.

THE PROBLEM OF PRACTICAL ECONOMIC PROBLEM SOLVING

By retaining the fundamental axiom that individual behavior is based on optimization, the classical objective to maximize wealth or market value may be seen as the overriding goal of economic behavior. However, within a complex, dynamically changing, uncertain, and multidimensional environment, the classical market approach to solving economic problems becomes increasingly suspect. Not only do the classical idealizations become increasingly unrealistic, but most practical problem situations do not have simple optimal solutions. Instead a multitude of different strategies exists to reach a particular goal in terms of different trade-off possibilities that can be considered. As soon as problems become more involved, the necessary knowledge and the required information may not be available to optimize. Under these circumstances, practical problem solving becomes more readily identified with an experimental learning process.

When a *systemic approach* to view practical economic problem solving is adopted, the limitations of the classical solution-oriented analytic approach becomes apparent. This is especially important in economic macrosystems based on credit money and where interest rates are controlled by monetary authorities. Under such circumstances, a long-run natural equilibrium interest rate does not exist. Furthermore, in the Keynesian model, it is the role of governments to manage economic affairs. Within managed economic systems, the economic environment is largely determined by government policies, so that a long-run equilibrium must be seen purely as a conceptual framework. Thus, the classical ideal of self-regulating market forces which will bring an economic system into a natural long-run equilibrium state must be questioned. Also, if we acknowledge that atomistic markets do not exist and that market participants are unique and different, then market equilibrium criteria apply only to marginal market participants.

As soon as the classical assumptions do not apply, for whatever reason, the benefits of the classical market equilibrium analysis become restricted to marginal market participants. In particular, for nonmarginal market participants: value $\neq$ price. This condition is discussed in the literature in terms of a consumer and producer surplus, whereby some individuals may gain substantial psychic values beyond the established market price. Furthermore, for individual economic entities, the cost of borrowing will be dependent on the size of the loan, so that: average prices $\neq$ marginal prices. Under these conditions, practical financial problem solving and market optimization criteria apply only to a marginal analysis. When individuals and problem situations become more unique and interdependent, then analytic approaches based on independence and separation principles, the value additivity principle, and a perfect market equilibrium may not hold. In a systemic interrelated environment, analytic simplifications become artificial and optimization criteria restricted to simple, structured, and well-defined problem situations.

While the benefits of analytic simplifications may outweigh logical inconsistencies within a *pragmatic view* of management, there are a large number of practical management problems that cannot be treated within the simplified and structured framework of a long-run equilibrium analysis. Whenever problem situations become more interrelated, they may not be artificially simplified, separated, and treated in isolation. In practical financial management, interdependencies require management procedures and financial strategies that recognize a larger perspective of dynamic changes. Within the accounting model, interrelatedness is recognized through accounting procedures, and within management models, through the design of organizational structures and the use of specific management procedures. Practical financial management involves procedures that recognize asset-liability management procedures that are controlled by asset-liability committees.

The analytic benefits of a *long-run equilibrium analysis* do not apply to short-term economic problem solving. While the definition of what constitutes a *short-term problem* is not clear, it is the assumption that market prices do not change in the short term which provides the basis for a short-term analysis. For a scalper trading on the floor of an exchange, a long-term investment position may refer to anything longer than one minute, while for other individuals it may involve a time horizon of longer than ten years. Thus, the definitions of short-term vs. long-term problem solving are unique to a particular economic agent. If we consider financial problem solving outside of the analytic simplifications of a long-run equilibrium analysis, then separation principles may not hold, so that the overall financial position has to be analyzed for an economic entity viewed as a whole.

Recognizing the volatility of financial markets makes a short-term market equilibrium analysis a questionable tool for practical financial problem solving. This relates especially to models that are based on assumed certainty or determinism. Recognition of short-term price fluctuations introduces the *concept of risk*. Therefore, practical problem solving must address the question of how much risk-exposure should be retained and how much should be hedged. Since risk-exposures involve different time horizons, the question of practical financial management becomes a matter of a *dynamic balance* between various aspects. In financial market equilibrium models, this trade-off is commonly treated in terms of expected returns and risks which are reflected in market equilibrium prices. By utilizing a long-run equilibrium analysis, individual economic entities adjust passively to market-given prices based on their individual risk-return preference. Financial positions must be constantly adjusted by acknowledging dynamically changing market conditions.

Such *dynamic adjustments* may involve individual financial positions or the whole balance sheet. Hedges can be lifted temporarily to take advantage of anticipated speculative gains. Thus, financial management becomes a matter of dynamic adjustments actively pursued as a matter of financial strategy. Instead of attaining a long-run mechanical equilibrium by adjusting passively to a long-run market equilibrium, the financial position of unique economic entities is adapted to new and changing environmental conditions. Thus, practical financial management becomes a matter of dynamic adjustments involving strategies of risk management and strategies of growth, stability, and speculation based on individual preferences. The market provides a large number of available contractual alternatives from which unique and different economic entities can choose, dependent on their specific problem situation.

Given the conclusions of a long-run market equilibrium analysis with atomistic economic entities pursuing their own self-interest of wealth optimization, then excess economic profits can be made only by retaining competitive advantages. Thus, a major goal of economic problem solving by individual economic entities is related to strategies that prevent the classical market ideal from taking effect. Through the *creation of barriers* to free competition, it is possible to retain excess profit opportunities. This possibility required government policies to assure competitive markets. Specific strategies that prevent free market competition involve restricted access to information, capital resources, and technology, as well as institutional arrangements that include such things as: patent laws, zoning laws, licensing requirements, membership provisions, duty barriers, tax provisions and other regulatory restrictions.

While the holder of specific privileges will rarely complain, it is the disenfranchised who will use social, political, legal, and economic processes to gain fair access to markets, information, technology, and economic resources by demanding a "level playing field." Thus, practical problem solving involves a whole array of approaches and processes which are dependent on specific strategies, goals, and situations, as well as on the ability and power to affect change.

THE ANALYTIC APPROACH TO PRACTICAL ECONOMIC PROBLEM SOLVING

By utilizing the analytic approach to problem simplifications in conjunction with the concept of a long-run equilibrium, it is possible to analyze specific aspects of financial problems in isolation. In particular, by assuming that long-run equilibrium conditions are natural and known, individuals can readily utilize the opportunity cost principle with respect to the market equilibrium in order to gain temporary excess economic profits. It is this process of exploiting opportunity costs which will bring an ideal classical economic system into a long-run equilibrium state. Practical economic problem solving becomes, therefore, a matter of applying rational methods to identify and to eliminate any market-related opportunity costs. Specific long-run market equilibrium criteria may help in this analysis, based on the Law of One Price and on criteria of optimal resource allocation. In the short run, by assuming that market prices remain fixed either through the use of contractual agreements or hedging procedures, practical economic problem solving is associated with the reduction of inefficiencies, the improvement of management procedures, and the use of operating methods which improve cost-benefit relations.

Whenever problem statements are well specified and structured, it is possible to identify specific classes of problems to which specific solution methods can be applied. This type of practical problem solving is associated with *engineering-type problems,* where sufficient experience and knowledge exists so that particular models properly reflect the problems. Within this framework, the task of a practicing problem solver or decisionmaker is associated with the discovery of the appropriate analogy between an actual problem situation and a specific problem class to which a solution method exists. All that is needed, after a particular solution method has been identified, is to accumulate the required, necessary, and relevant information. Since any mathematical manipulation of data and equations can be performed better by computers, it is the belief in such *rational problem-solving approaches* that has led to the development of a vast array of computer software packages. All that is needed to solve practical financial problems is access to relevant information and a computer terminal.

When problems become increasingly complex, interrelated, multidimensional, and dynamically changing, the required information may not be available and the required knowledge may not exist. In such situations practical problem solving is more appropriately associated with *experimental learning processes*. Instead of applying models based on abstract idealizations and analytic simplifications, the systemic interrelatedness is recognized explicitly. Available contractual alternatives are used in order to find an acceptable balance among the multitude of circumstances affecting the economic conditions of a specific economic entity. Within this view, practical financial management becomes a means to actively pursue strategies in order to attain specific objectives. If we recognize the time required to affect environmental change, then much of the repositioning of financial positions is associated with processes, procedures, and policies. Acknowledging the dynamically changing environmental conditions in which economic entities operate makes practical financial and economic problem solving a matter of pursuing dynamic strategies instead of finding optimal solutions to well-specified problem statements.

It is this aspect of practical financial management which separates the practical domain of financial management from the theoretical domain of finance research. Both areas pursue different goals, use different models and ideas, and address different aspects of economic problem solving. It is the adherence to the analogy with mechanical physics and engineering-type problem-solving that has governed the area of financial management for a long time. Different practical problem-solving approaches have evolved more recently, by people adopting a more systemic view.

THE EVOLUTION OF DIFFERENT PROBLEM-SOLVING APPROACHES

Without going into any detail or following any strict chronological order, we briefly outline some of the changing characteristics of practical economic problem-solving approaches that have evolved over time. Based on the fundamental postulate that human behavior is goal-directed and optimizing (Bentham), the classical economic model introduced the framework of perfect atomistic competitive markets and the concept of a long-run equilibrium to derive a normative model of the free market ideal (Adam Smith). By embracing the principles of individual freedom, private property rights, and self-detemined pursuit of happiness, the normative values implied by the free market ideal also have provided the foundation of accepted social and political values. Adopting classical economic models for practical problem solving also has changed the fundamental concept of economic model building over time.

Classical economic models utilize the analogy with mechanical physics as introduced by Newton and the analytic-deductive approach to scientific model building as formulated by Aristotle. During the twentieth century the basic principles underlying the nineteenth-century mechanical physics have been revised, which has affected also the interpretation of classical economic models. While the acceptance of *new views* by the general public is slow, the evolutionary change is reflected in new practical problem-solving approaches. As part of this evolutionary change, it is the belief in independent atomistic elements of nature that was augmented by a concern for systemic interrelationships. The belief in determinism and optimality was replaced by statistical uncertainty, and the concept of a stable static mechanical equilibrium was modified by a concern for systemic balance and dynamic adaptation. Recognition of a more complex and multidimensional environment with systemic interrelationships also changed the belief in the fixed cause-effect relationships. This evolutionary change in beliefs is not restricted to physics or economics, but it permeates all fields of knowledge, including medicine, biology, or even astronomy. New fields of study evolved, such as ecology, cybernetics, electronics, and bionics. As a consequence, the old established order of things and their fixed relationships has also been questioned in social-economic systems. This, in turn, affects the practical domain of financial management and accepted ways of practical economic problem solving.

As the view of problems faced by *practitioners* changes, the practitioners will adopt new problem-solving approaches as well as new organizational management systems. While the belief in the virtues of the classical free-market model is still strong, new problem-solving approaches have evolved over time which recognize more completely the concept of systemic interrelationships. The adoption of new management approaches has also changed the classical view of financial management. The fixed decision rules based on passive adjustments to the market equilibrium conditions were altered to reflect more closely the active strategies that are pursued in order to cope with ever-changing environmental conditions. To trace this *evolutionary change,* we identify the nine following problem-solving approaches:

1. *The long-run atomistic market equilibrium approach.* Given that free economic systems tend to evolve toward a stable long-run equilibrium state, then long-run equilibrium prices can be used to evaluate economic alternatives. By following the market rule, individual economic agents can evaluate decision alternatives with respect to the market equilibrium, and they will optimize by eliminating all market-related opportunity costs. Since market equilibrium criteria are based on optimization rules with *fixed prices,* the atomistic market assumptions and rational behavior will guarantee separation principles, value additivity, and the Law of One Price. The opportunity cost principle, based on determinism and complete knowledge, provides clear criteria for practical economic problem solving. By utilizing specific analytic simplifications, the *market rule* implies structured mathematical optimization rules. These structured rules can be applied within the practical domain of financial management to solve all kinds of financial problems, as discussed in Part II.

2. *The scientific management and cost-accounting approach.* Concerned with the lack of efficient management procedures and outright waste of scarce economic resources, Frederick Taylor introduced cost measurements and mathematical models to improve practical management procedures. By using scientific methods and cost-accounting procedures, it is possible to optimize specific

operating conditions by minimizing costs, given *known prices*. A large number of mathematical optimization models have been developed over time, including linear programming as well as nonlinear programming methods. The importance of such mathematical procedures is based on the assumption that mathematical statements reflect the structure and processes implied by the real problem to be solved. This concept follows *engineering-type problem solving*, where problems are structured and where sufficient knowledge exists to verify specific models. The economic benefit of such scientific management models is based on the detection and elimination of opportunity costs that are incurred because of nonoptimal operating procedures. The practical value of such models is critically dependent on the correspondence of the model with actual problems faced by practitioners. Practical applications are largely restricted to well-defined and structured problem situations, such as scheduling, maintenance, inventory, and production problems in the short run.

3. *Statistical and probabilistic approaches.* As the required information needed to solve specific mathematical models becomes more uncertain because of measurement problems, stochastic processes, or future relatedness, probabilistic estimation procedures can be introduced. The structure of underlying mathematical models is largely retained. Only the required information is treated in terms of probabilistic estimates. Probabilistic solution techniques require, however, specific *trade-off relationships* which account for the existence of risk. While there are various approaches that account for risk-return trade-offs, it is the classical market approach which provides equilibrium measures of a *market price of risk,* based on risk diversification defined in standard mean-variance models or in linear regression models. These statistical market equilibrium models utilize the classical atomistic market assumptions and thereby maintain the classical problem-solving approaches. Given known risk classes for all decision alternatives, it is the objective of practical problem solving to eliminate any market-related, risk-adjusted opportunity costs. A market equilibrium

is based on fixed criteria which can be exploited by utilizing the Law of One Price or the elimination of arbitrage opportunities.

4. *The efficient market approach.* By introducing the concept that financial markets are perfect information processors, current prices in financial markets will be in an *informational equilibrium* that reflects all publicly available information. The essence of this proposition is stated in terms of the efficient market hypothesis. *Current market prices* will reflect the appropriate risk-adjusted equilibrium opportunity cost of money associated with specific financial contracts traded in the market. This approach maintains all the benefits of the classical market equilibrium approach. However, the long-run equilibrium concept is replaced by a concept of *continuous equilibrium* based on rational expectations. Given market-determined equilibrium prices, individual economic agents adjust passively to the market and thereby optimize by following the market rule. Given the initial wealth of an economic entity, the objective is to eliminate all market-related opportunity costs.

The *current market equilibrium concept* differs from the classifical long-run equilibrium approach. If we recognize the importance of information on equilibrium prices, then the link between market prices and classical optimization rules becomes weak. If market prices reflect nonoptimal resource allocations within a particular firm, then these market prices *cannot* be used to make *allocation decisions*. Thus, a firm should use the market equilibrium risk-adjusted opportunity cost to evaluate decision alternatives and not their own existing average-weighted cost of capital, which is only relevant if the market reflects a long-run equilibrium. A firm optimizes market values by eliminating all market-related opportunity costs. Thus, the practical implications for economic problem solving follow the classical market approach.

The *efficient market hypothesis* highlights the dependence of market prices on information randomly entering the market. By assuming stable stochastic processes generating new information, the observed random fluctuation of ''equilibrium'' market prices becomes also a stable random process. By utilizing statistical time series models, a stable risk-adjusted opportunity cost of money can be determined from ex post data. A decision analysis follows classical equilibrium criteria based on the market rule and the opportunity cost principle.

5. *The strategic management approach.* If we recognize more of the multidimensional interrelationships among systemic problems, then practical problem solving becomes associated with specific goals, missions, or objectives to be attained. The systemic complexity and the lack of basic knowledge replaces quantitative optimization models with methods of qualitative analysis and management control processes. Problems must be analyzed not only by their own structure, but also with respect to their impact on environmental conditions. Government projects, for example, require the assessment of impacts on environmental conditions in terms of environmental impact studies. In general, such problem-solving approaches are readily identified with *management models* that address management procedures and processes to actively plan and control the success of a particular project.

By recognizing *active control* over the success of a particular project through employee motivation, marketing strategies, and advertising campaigns as well as through flexible adaptation to new and changing environmental conditions, this problem-solving approach replaces the passive market rule with *active management procedures.* Specific strategies to enhance the competitive advantage are treated in this approach. For this purpose, all alternatives to gain competitive advantages are utilized, ranging from government subsidies and protection to the creation of market barriers and informational constraints. As a practical approach to economic problem solving, the passive adjustment to eliminate market opportunity costs is replaced by actively eliminating any opportunity costs associated with foregoing *profit-enhancing strategies.* This may include the opportunity cost associated with not lobbying for government protection. Thus, practical economic problem solving utilizes all aspects of preventing the classical market model from working as postulated.

It should be remembered that the free-market ideal was introduced as a normative model to be implemented and supported by governments in order to gain the benefits associated with the model. By assuming that the free market ideal already exists or that long-run equilibrium prices are known by all atomistic market participants, we can apply the postulated market rules to solve practical economic problems. However, any significant departure from the idealizing assumptions underlying the classical market model may lead to nonpractical problem-solving procedures.

6. *The management control systems approach.* In contrast to classical market equilibrium approaches where prices and quantities are fixed by assumed equilibrium conditions, the management control approach recognizes the impact of *fluctuating prices* and quantities on production, inventory, and employment. To actively respond to changing environmental conditions, different strategies and policies are used, for example, to maintain uniform production rates. This policy may affect inventory and employment levels, as well as pricing strategies, marketing strategies, and the characteristics of production methods and technology. By considering an *adaptive approach* to changing environmental conditions as an ongoing process, management control procedures plan and monitor the performance of various aspects of the economic entity. Opportunity costs are determined with respect to a plan and are controlled through management procedures. Thus, optimization models are replaced by practical management procedures (satisficing models).

Special *computer-supported management control systems* were developed in the 1970s. In particular, material requirement planning systems (MRP) not only plan and schedule production, but also control inventory levels and coordinate purchasing and marketing strategies, as well as integrate engineering and finance. These computer systems are used to generate management reports, simulate "what-if" scenarios, analyze future capacity extensions, and evaluate new production technologies and management procedures. The organizational system is viewed as a *complete whole*, and all activities are coordinated through management plans, budgets, and plan reviews. Thus, practical economic problem solving becomes a matter of continuous management processes.

7. *The cooperative systems approach.* Classical economic models are based on the principle of competition among relatively small atomistic economic entities. It is the profit motive together with competition which will lead to lower prices, efficient use of scarce resources, and optimal allocation of resources, as well as a long-run equilibrium state. Since competitive market systems also result in uncertainty, risk, and instability, they lead to fluctuating inventory and employment levels.

A cooperative systems approach to solve practical economic problems explicitly recognizes systemic interdependencies among different economic entities. Through cooperation, scheduling, and high-quality standards, it is possible to reduce inventory levels and production costs. A particular cooperative approach is associated with the *Just in Time (JIT)* manufacturing systems, which involve suppliers, producers, and distributors. In a cooperative system, the management practices involve concepts that differ drastically from classical competitive approaches. As a comprehensive philosophy, JIT manufacturing is founded on principles that involve teamwork, quality circle programs, multiskilled workers, life-long employment, committment to total quality, proactive maintenance, and continuous improvement. By recognizing that for many products and nonclassical atomistic markets "Value $\neq$ Price" for all nonmarginal market participants, we see that performance is not measured only by price, but by other things such as quality, dependability, and availability. Cooperative systems collaborate internally in order to achieve competitive advantages for facing other economic entities in market competition. While various forms of cooperative systems exist, it is the free-market ideal as a normative model which prohibits such arrangements.

Opportunity cost is recognized as any deviation from some *ideal competitive advantage* and is continuously reduced through improvements in production methods and management procedures, as well as cooperation and government support. As such, the creation of value is seen as a continuous and adaptive process that requires participation, commitment, and continuous learning. Instead of relying on anonymous market forces, the reduction of opportunity costs requires active management and motivated individuals.

8. *The human system approach.* Classical economic models treat human beings purely as an economic resource that is priced in competitive markets according to their marginal productivity. As such, individuals are treated in terms of homogeneous populations that represent replaceable parts. Individual differences and unique human characteristics are ignored.

The human system approach to practical problem solving recognizes the complex nature of human organizations, and it views problem solving as an *experimental learning process.* Instead of implementing rational, scientific, engineering-type solutions to analytic and simplified problem statements based on questionable measurements, the human system approach explicitly recognizes the importance of *human individuality.* Thus, the belief in atomistic equality is replaced by individual diversity. The belief in harmonious agreement among rational individuals leading to stable mechanistic equilibrium conditions and consensus-pricing processes is augmented by the recognition of conflicts among different individuals. Instead of being ignored, *conflicts* are utilized to discover new problems and new solution approaches. Thus, practical solutions to human problems are developed through processes that recognize the complex, interrelated, and multidimensional nature of human organizations.

Opportunity costs do not exist as clearly defined measurable quantitites with respect to some long-run market equilibrium, but they involve psychic values and individual preferences that differ among different human beings. The goal of the human system approach is the development of processes and environments to make it possible for different individuals to reduce their own *individual* opportunity costs. Human beings as individuals should be able to achieve their full potential. Practical economic problem solving utilizes the know-how and experience of all involved individuals through *participatory* problem-solving processes, which in organizations may involve such things as brainstorming sessions, suggestion boxes, and synectics.

9. *The generalized opportunity cost principle approach.*
Classical economic models are concerned with long-run market
equilibrium states to derive criteria which determine optimal
resource allocations based on such ideals as complete rationality,
atomistic markets, full knowledge, and determinism. As such, these
models do not address organizational systems, individual diversity,
complex interdependencies, institutional and environmental
changes, and the multitude of processes to maintain competitive
advantages in order to earn excess economic profits. As a normative model, the free-market concept was originally introduced
as an ideal to be pursued in order to gain the advantages of individual freedom, property rights, and the freedom of choice.

By emphasizing the scientific interpretation of the free-market
model, the testing of empirical propositions and market equilibrium
criteria became an important part of the theoretical domain of
finance. By calling attention to the necessity to maintain competitive
advantages for business organizations, government institutions,
as well as municipalities, states, and countries, the need to manage
all types of economic and human affairs became an important part
of the practical domain of financial management. During the nineteenth century the free-market ideal became an accepted ideal to
be pursued, as reflected by the gold standard, the antitrust laws,
and the democratization of governments. After World War I and
the Great Depression of the 1930s, new ideas developed as reflected
by Keynesian economics, concepts of social responsibility, and
the need to control the quantity of credit money. In conjunction
with the change of the mechanical view of the universe in physics,
during the twentieth century a new view evolved that recognizes
the need to acknowledge systemic interrelationships as well as
systemic complexities.

All that evolutionary change brought about drastic technological
advances and a continuing change in the environmental conditions.
While the normative ideal of the free-market model introduced
in the nineteenth century highlights the importance of individual
rights, it is the concern for *individual opportunities* that is addressed
in the twentieth century. To create an environment and processes

so that individuals can reach their fullest potential requires a change in the existing organizational structures, institutional arrangements, and accepted methods, processes, and procedures for practical problem solving. Individuals attempting to reduce their own individual opportunity costs should be able to utilize their particular abilities and unique individual characteristics. As part of this evolutionary change, work arrangements include flexible working hours, home work stations, and individualized entrepreneurship. While institutional barriers and laws against such flexibility exist, it is the creation of new choices in the work place and the market place which reduces institutionalized barriers to employment, education, and human services.

For practical problem solving, the *generalized opportunity cost principle* approach provides a normative ideal based on individualism and freedom of choice. Individuals, by attempting to reach their fullest potential, are reducing individual opportunity costs through the *freedom of choice.* By providing more choice alternatives in the market place and by eliminating institutional barriers, the free-market ideal still provides the fundamental criteria for normative values. If we recognize the multitude of individual differences, then the existing concept of homogeneous equality and stable mechanical equilibrium criteria must seem to be obsolete principles that are based on analytic simplifications to artificially reduce the beautiful complexity and diversity of a systemically interrelated world.

These various and different *approaches to practical problem solving* reflect the dichotomy between the analytic and the systemic approach to view and solve problems. Furthermore, these different approaches highlight the critical assumptions on which practical solutions are based. While normative models present guidelines and arguments to change existing organizational and institutional arrangements, it is the existing structure that distributes benefits and costs to individuals within a social, political, and economic human organizational system. It is the interrelatedness of political, legal, social, and economic processes that affects the ability of specific individuals to reduce their own subjectively determined opportunity cost by utilizing available market choices. Thus, it is the systemic view of human organizations which will guide human systems design in the future, with the goal to provide increasingly more market opportunities and freedom of choice.

A PROCESS VIEW OF PRACTICAL FINANCIAL PROBLEM SOLVING

Different problem-solving approaches reflect different views of the environment in which problems are defined. As such, practical financial management may utilize different approaches to address different problem situations. Within the analytic view specific problems are identified and solved in isolation, while the systemic view treats problems as an integral part of an organizational system. By utilizing the concept of a market equilibrium, individual economic entities adjust their financial structure passively by following the market rule in order to optimize their market value. Since market equilibrium conditions imply that no changes occur, financial problem solving is treated within a static or stable stationary environment. By employing the assumption of perfect markets, the present value method can be used to convert future expected cash flows into a measure of equivalent current value. This approach is based on the opportunity cost of money as a measure of the time-value associated with money.

To utilize the analytic view of problem solving, basic assumptions are introduced to gain specific benefits. For example, to apply *analytic-type* problem-solving approaches, it is assumed that:

1. Individuals are essentially all equally pursuing the same economic goal of wealth maximization
2. Problems can be treated within analytic separation principles
3. Optimal solutions can be found through precise solution methods and the measurements of critical variables
4. The environment approaches stable and well-defined equilibrium conditions

By contrast, systemic-type problem-solving approaches recognize the complex interdependencies among different problem situations within a dynamically changing environment. Market prices react to new information so that interactions exist between market prices and decisions within a firm. This link does not exist in a static long-run equilibrium analysis. By acknowledging the dynamic adjustment of prices to changing environmental conditions, problem solving is more readily associated with an experimental learning process. Instead of finding optimal solutions to well-specified problem statements, problem solving becomes a continuous process of adapting to changing environmental conditions affected by new regulations, new tax laws, and changes in the competitive market environment. Since excess economic profits can be gained through competitive advantages, much of the problem-solving process is concerned with maintaining and creating such advantages. By recognizing the nature of market-pricing processes, individuals can gain excess profits in the market through insider information and trading schemes. These *market manipulations* are largely illegal and may involve complex schemes including takeover bids and the cornering of markets. Within the systemic view, practical financial management becomes more than a passive application of market rules and rational optimization methods, and it is readily associated with active financial strategies and management control processes. In particular, *systemic-type* problem-solving approaches are based on a set of assumptions that include:

1. Individuals are unique and different with respect to their goals and aspirations

2. Problem situations are viewed with respect to their systemic interrelationships

3. There are no optimal solutions but only processes which are controlled by specific strategies

4. The environment is continuously changing and individuals are adapting to new conditions

Recognizing the different views of problem solving in the systemic and analytic approaches, practical management procedures will differ in each area. In financial management, these different views will affect problem definitions as well as problem-solution approaches. For example, within the analytic view of rational financial management there is the concern with such things as:

1. Finding the optimal asset, capital, and debt structure by analyzing accounting statements in terms of specific values and ratios. Utilizing the concept of homogeneous industries, individuals can compare ratios to accepted industry averages. Such a method is based on the beliefs that rational decisionmakers will always optimize and that individual differences are randomly distributed (the Law of Large Numbers), so that averages can be used to guide decisionmakers.

2. Analyzing new investment opportunities and existing projects with respect to market-determined equilibrium prices. By eliminating any market-related opportunity costs, economic entities can optimize their market value. This method is based on the belief that markets reflect long-run equilibrium conditions or at least that short-run equilibrium conditions are stable during the time horizon relevant for the analysis. As such, these methods ignore the dynamic nature of competitive markets.

3. Determining mispriced market opportunities to exploit excess economic profits. By following classical market equilibrium criteria, arbitrage positions can be exploited. These approaches ignore the possibility that markets reflect other pricing processes than those implied by complete rationality.

4. Determining any inefficiencies or misallocated resources with respect to the market by following the market rule. This approach uses established market equilibrium criteria to detect unexploited opportunity costs.

Within the *accounting model,* such problem-solving approaches are related to the improvement of accounting income by analyzing decision alternatives in terms of explicit costs and benefits. By recognizing the impact of implicit costs and opportunity costs, in addition to explicit costs and benefits, accounting data should be adjusted to reflect market and cash-flow-related information. Similarly, the analysis of balance sheet data to analyze liquidity, risk, and return relationships should be corrected for market values. In addition, a financial analysis of accounting data should recognize any contractual arrangements that are off the balance sheet and that affect the financial position of a firm. This introduces the problem that certain contractual arrangements are considered private information. Thus, executory contracts, hedging positions, and risk exposures are not reported. Specific assets such as patents, human knowledge, and technological advances which provide competitive advantages also may not be reflected in accounting data. Therefore, any analysis of financial accounting data is an art more than a rational procedure.

While the *practical domain* of financial management recognizes the complex and dynamically changing environmental conditions by utilizing process-oriented management procedures, the *theoretical domain* utilizes simple analytic models to discover natural laws that govern such practical management processes. By utilizing scientific methods and analytic model building based on fundamental assumptions that simplify an otherwise complex reality, the theoretical domain has embraced the concept of a stable market equilibrium. Within this approach, it is possible to test specific propositions or to discover stable relationships among particular variables and measurements. It is the analogy with methods applied in natural sciences and mechanical physics that has guided this approach. While the theoretical domain gains particular benefits from simplifying a complex reality, the practical domain cannot ignore the specific characteristics and dynamic interdependencies of a particular problem situation.

STRATEGIC FINANCIAL MANAGEMENT

The goal to maintain competitive advantages and to earn excess economic profits recognizes the need to compete not only on prices but also in terms of quality, availability, and flexibility. In terms of financial management this requires the adaptation of financial positions to an ever-changing environment and the treatment of specific, unique, and different problem situations. Thus, practical financial management must acknowledge the impact of dynamic changes, the effect of a general lack of knowledge, as well as the possibility of unforeseen events. For this reason, practitioners utilize a variety of different approaches to practical problem solving. Depending on the particular circumstances, such problem-solving approaches may involve specific strategies to deal with threats and opportunities associated with conditions such as hostile takeover bids, competitive price changes, regulatory and tax changes, as well as technological advances or attempts to monopolize a market. To respond properly, financial management must be aware of possible alternatives to meet particular problem situations. Depending on the particular circumstances and the economic entity involved, responses may include legal, legislative, and political actions as well as economic, social, and military sanctions. Thus, practical financial management must deal with the social, political, and economic system as a whole.

Depending on the specific objectives, goals, and mission statements of a particular economic entity, modern financial markets provide a wide variety of alternatives to pursue different financial strategies. Specific strategies may involve:

1. Simple contractual arrangements involving long-term debt and equity claims
2. Different short-term loan agreements such as credit lines, revolving credit, or standby credit based on various procedures to pledge or sell collateral
3. The selling of short-term securities in the open market to raise short-term funds directly through commercial papers or certificates of deposit
4. Different financing involving off balance sheet arrangements such as leasing, sales lease-back, or leveraged leases
5. Hedging positions involving options, futures, options on futures, or index futures

6. Arbitrage positions to gain risk-free returns

7. Speculative positions to take advantage of market moves in the right direction

8. Different pricing and trading rules

Specific strategies may also involve contractual arrangements to change financial positions in response to environmental changes resulting in different risk exposures or ownership relations. Such arrangements may include foreign currencies, the timing of cash receipts and expenditures, variable or fixed financing, and contingency contracts. In particular, such strategies may involve financial arrangements that increase the flexibility to adjust financial positions as well as liquidity to finance growth of service activities. New strategies involve such things as:

1. Pooling. This refers to the creation of a pool of assets and the issuing of "pass-through" securities by which ownership rights and cash income are passed on to the holder of such securities. This provides for participatory financing arrangements and removes assets from the balance sheet of individual economic entities.

2. Securitization. This refers to the selling of claims against specific assets, mainly bank loans, in terms of collateralized financial obligations. In particular, new innovative securities have been created such as "interest income only" or "principal payment only" securities. Such securities are guaranteed by some guarantor, which removes the risk associated with the underlying assets.

3. Swap arrangements. There are essentially two types of swaps—interest rate and currency. Two parties agree, for example, to exchange floating-rate debt for fixed-rate debt, or one currency for another. Swap arrangements may be made contingent on certain events known as "swaptions" and allow for a rapid adjustment of financial positions.

4. Defeasance. This is a debt-restructuring tool that enables a firm to remove debt from its balance sheet by establishing an irrevocable trust holding securities that will generate future cash flows sufficient to service the debt.

Specific strategies exist that address a broad range of consequences of various transactions to initiate takeover attempts. Strategies also exist to resist takeover attempts, which also may involve many different aspects. These defensive strategies are described in such colorful terms as "scorched earth," "poision pill," "golden parachutes," as well as "greenmail," "white knights," and "doomsday defense." There are strategies which address ownership arrangements through partnerships, joint ventures, subsidiary arrangements, and licensing. In addition, there are strategies to develop new markets, new products, and new production technology, as well as strategies to enter foreign markets or for developing access to new resources. It is the systemic view of economic problem solving which treats the need to coordinate different strategies in order to manage the business affairs of an economic entity as an integrated whole.

While a multitude of different strategies exist to be pursued by different and unique economic entities with the goal to attain specific objectives, it is the *opportunity cost principle* that guides the selection of specific strategies. Given that such a selection process can also be analyzed within the analytic model of rational choice, it is the systemic view of interrelated problem situations that determines the selection of any specific strategy in practical problem solving. Instead of searching for optimal strategies, individuals should recognize the complexity of interrelated systems, the general lack of knowledge, and the nonexistence of stable long-run equilibrium conditions which associate strategic management with an experimental learning process. Within the framework of the general opportunity cost principle, individual differences and the unique characteristics of specific problem situations can be recognized within the specific objectives to be attained. Recognizing the dynamic nature of the economic, political, and social environment of human organizations, the *generalized opportunity cost principle* can be expressed as: The rational objective of any economic entity is a process of continuously reducing individualized opportunity costs.

OPPORTUNITY COST AND COMPUTERIZED DECISION SUPPORT SYSTEMS

A decision support system (DSS) is essentially a computer-based management tool, designed to aid specific individuals in their own unique decision-making processes. As such, a DSS does not solve any specific problem, but supports individuals in their own judgmental processes to analyze problem situations and to develop a strategy to address a resolution to the problem. Thus, instead of providing a set of rigid rules and mathematical solution methods to solve specific structured and well-defined problem statements, a DSS represents a flexible, interactive computer system, with access to various data files and different computer programs. The objective of a DSS is to provide easy routines to utilize computers in the process of bringing *value-adding ideas* into an organization. For this purpose, computers may be interlinked to provide better means to coordinate and facilitate the many processes by which organizations develop new ideas, manage their operation, and adapt to new environmental conditions.

By recognizing the particular characteristics of different organizations and the specific abilities of unique individuals, it is possible to address special problem situations and novel problem aspects defined within a complex, interrelated and dynamically changing environment. It is this concern which is supported by DSS as a new type of *flexible management tool*. As such, a DSS may be utilized in specific applications within particular organizational functions such as new product design, proactive maintenance procedures, total quality assurance, accounting, and financial management. It is the adaptability of a DSS to any particular application area which separates a DSS from traditional mathematical problem-solution methods that solve specific structured and well-defined problem statements.

By switching from the analytic approach of problem solving applied within the framework of structured engineering-type problem statements to the systemic approach which addresses processes of experimental learning, continuous improvement, and adaptation to new environmental conditions, it is the *generalized opportunity cost principle* which defines the objective of such rational processes. While in the mechanistic-analytic approach, humans are viewed as economic resources that can be replaced by machines in an effort to optimize an owner's wealth or market value, it is the systemic view which recognizes the unique abilities of humans to reason, to handle complex problem situations, and to adapt to change.

Instead of concentrating on wealth optimization as the sole objective of human behavior, we see that it is the reduction of ever-changing opportunity costs that motivates unique and different individuals. If we acknowledge a general hierarchy of human needs (see Figure 6.1) as postulated by Maslow, then we reduce the importance of material needs as the motivating force. A large percentage of today's work force views work as more than a means of economic survival, and many *theories of motivation* recognize higher levels of human needs.

The economic value of a DSS, therefore, is based on the specific circumstances for which it is used and the particular abilities of individuals who use it. While traditional approaches are concerned with the *efficiency* of using economic resources, including human labor, it is the concern with *effectiveness* that is addressed by DSS. Instead of viewing machines and computers as a means to replace humans in an effort to reduce explicit costs, we can see that it is the contribution of such new machines that frees individuals from the drudgery of repetitive work. Thus, it is possible to discover and reduce existing opportunity costs associated with individuals and organizations operating in larger interdependent socioeconomic systems. While in traditional economic models, machines replaced human labor as an economic resource, the emphasis in DSS is to support management and owners as decisionmakers. In this sense, a DSS does not replace labor to reduce explicit costs but to enhance profitability by eliminating opportunity costs.

It is the special role of a DSS as a management tool which has to be appreciated. To analyze the *economic value* of a DSS, individuals must recognize its full impact on the organizational

Figure 6.1
Maslow's Hierarchy of Needs

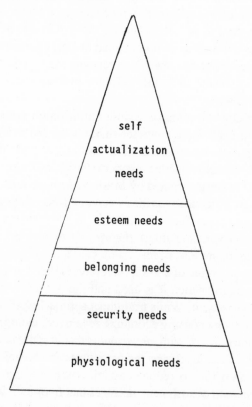

design, management philosophy, and management processes. The classical market equilibrium approach or the traditional analysis of explicit costs and benefits is insufficient. The full impact on the reduction of opportunity costs must be considered. Within a dynamically changing environment with unknown and *unexpected surprises*, it is the ability to react rapidly to new trends and opportunities which affect economic value. Instead of projecting long-run market equilibrium values or evaluating *static optimization criteria*, it is the concern for dynamic adaptation, flexibility, risk exposure, and competitive advantages that must be considered when assessing the economic value of a specific DSS. The economic value of a DSS must reflect its contribution to the continuous process of reducing opportunity costs.

By addressing unique individuals and organizations all operating within systemically interrelated environments, markets become a *reservoir of choice alternatives* instead of a reference point for assessing long-term market opportunity costs. Any individual or organization with unique and different requirements can choose freely from among the many alternatives available in the market. Within financial management this involves a wide variety of financial contracts which are available in the market and which can be used to pursue specific financial strategies. As such, the structuring of a financial position may involve equity contracts, short-term and long-term debt, various forms of contingent contracts such as options, futures, options on futures, or contingent swap arrangements (swaptions), as well as combinations, straddles, spreads, strips, and straps. The increasing variety of debt contracts, ranging from traditional fixed-rates to variable-rates and zero-coupon contracts, provides an environment that promotes different hedging and swap arrangements. The international dimension of closely interrelated financial markets highlights the wide variety of financial strategies that are available to address particular financial problem situations. In this complex environment the benefits of a particular financial DSS can be fully appreciated.

By acknowledging the *dynamic nature of financial management* and the unique differences among different organizations and individuals, we can appreciate the full complexity of financial management. In an individualized and dynamic environment, the limitations of assumed atomistic equality and static equilibrium conditions become apparent. Instead of passively following the market rule by eliminating market opportunity costs defined with respect to some assumed known, stable, and deterministic long-run equilibrium, some individuals faced with unique and various problem situations attempt to reduce their own *individual opportunity cost*. This involves not only subjective valuations and judgmental processes, but also measures of opportunity cost that include psychic values. As long as markets reflect equilibrium prices determined by marginal market participants, market prices do not reflect an appropriate measure of opportunity costs for all. Thus, nonmarginal market participants must assess their own individual situation preferences and opportunity costs. The dynamic change of market prices and individual problem situations requires a continuous adjustment. The process of a continuous reduction of changing opportunity costs is addressed by the generalized opportunity cost principle.

By emphasizing dynamic changes, complex systemic interrelationships, and limited knowledge, it is possible to identify *rational processes for problem solving*. Such processes are associated with continuous learning, experimentation, creativity, and the appreciation of unique and different individuals. Such ideas are also reflected in *accepted common wisdom* that exists besides mathematical rationality and fixed optimization rules. A few of these accepted ideas are such statements as:

- Don't fix what is not broken
- Work on important things first
- Use all the help you can get
- Understand the problem first
- Cover your down-side risk

These ideas conflict with *mathematical rationality* which defines rational problem solving in terms of a complete problem definition such as:

1. Analyze and value rank *all* feasible alternatives
2. Select the optimal alternative

It is a different objective which is treated by these approaches. While mathematical rationality is concerned with defining an optimal solution from a set of well-specified alternatives within a theory of rational choice, a rational process for problem solving is concerned with strategies to address complex, multidimensional and poorly defined problem situations within a dynamically changing environment.

While mathematical optimization models search for optimal solutions to well-specified and structured problem statements, it is the DSS approach which supports the *judgmental process* of practical problem solving. Classical economic theory discusses the conditions of an ideal, long-run, atomistic market equilibrium state to derive decision rules to optimally allocate scarce economic resources, based on the idea to eliminate long-run market opportunity costs. This leads to passive market rules to be followed. Instead, the concern of practical problem solving addresses the process of maintaining or gaining competitive advantages within a dynamically changing environment. For example, the development of new products emphasizes the process of discovering new ideas or the process of transferring an idea from a conceptual state to a final product to be sold. This *development process* involves pilot studies in engineering, marketing, and production. It is this process-oriented management approach which is supported by DSS. Depending on the particular functional area, we can identify specific DSS applications in terms of:

Computer-Aided Design (CAD), which provides interactive graphics that assist in the development of new products or the design of specific parts

Computer Testing of Prototypes, which uses computer simulations to test certain physical design characteristics of specific parts

Automated Drafting, which utilizes computer-stored data to make and change technical drawings

Computer-Aided Manufacturing (CAM), which uses computers to control processing or material-handling equipment

Computer-Integrated Manufacturing (CIM), which is a concept of linking and coordinating a broad array of activities through an integrated computer system

Expert Systems (ES), which make the knowledge of special experts available to other users within a particular field of interest

Artificial Intelligence (AI), which allows an automated manufacturing system to reconfigure itself without human intervention by emulating human methods of learning and problem solving

Electronic Data Interchange (EDI), which allows an efficient means to coordinate among different suppliers and users of parts, information, and plans

It is the special characteristics of a DSS as a management tool which distinguishes a DSS from other *machines*. While a clear separation between a DSS and a machine is dependent on the specific criteria applied, we define a DSS as a flexible tool that aids in decision making and mental processes, in contrast to a machine that performs specific mechanical functions. It is the combination of computers and machines together with artificial intelligence that has led to new types of machines known as *robots*. This new development has brought about the concept of flexible manufacturing systems, which involves such ideas as multiskilled workers, continuous improvement, participatory efforts, flexible scheduling, intermittent production runs, proactive maintenance, total quality control as well as Just in Time production methods. It is this *process-oriented view* which is distinct and different from analytic optimization models.

To assess the economic benefits of such flexible systems that readily adapt to environmental changes involves more than classical long-run market equilibrium models and fixed-market rules. It is an *active process* to create value, to maintain competitive advantages, and to continuously improve conditions within human systems. To assess the economic value of flexibility involves the needs and requirements of specific, unique, and different individuals. Economic value must consider the special circumstances that apply to a particular problem situation which should be viewed and analyzed with respect to the organizational environment in which it is placed. The value of a *timely response* to environmental changes and to unforeseen threats and opportunities can be evaluated only in terms of individualized opportunity costs. It is the concept of continuous improvement which is addressed by the generalized opportunity cost principle.

References

Accounting Principles Board. 1964. *Opinion No. 5.* "Reporting of Leases in Financial Statements of Lessee." American Institute of Certified Public Accountants. New York.

Accounting Principles Board. 1966. *Opinion No. 7.* "Accounting for Leases in Financial Statements of Lessors." American Institute of Certified Public Accountants. New York.

Accounting Principles Board. 1971. *Opinion No. 21.* "Interest on Receivables and Payables." American Institute of Certified Public Accounts. New York.

Akers, M. D. 1986, Fall. "Opportunity Costs in the Accounts." *The Accounting Historians Notebook.*

Archer, S. and C. A. D'Ambrosio. 1966. *Business Finance: Theory and Management.* New York: Macmillan.

Arrow, K. 1964a. "The Role of Securities in the Optimal Allocation of Risk Bearing." *Review of Economic Studies,* pp. 91–96.

Arrow, K. 1964b. *Essays in the Theory of Risk Bearing.* New York: American Elsevier Publishing Company.

Baxter, W. T. 1975. *Accounting Values and Inflation.* London: McGraw-Hill.

Bertalanffy, von, L. 1971. *General Systems Theory.* Harmondsworth, Middlesex: Penguin Books.

Bierman, H. 1963. *Topics in Cost Accounting and Decisions.* New York: McGraw-Hill.

Bierman, H. and T. Dyckman. 1976. *Managerial Cost Accounting,* 2nd ed. New York: Macmillan.

Bierman, H. and T. Dyckman. 1980. *The Capital Budgeting Decision,* 5th ed. New York: Macmillan.

Bloom, R. and A. Debessay. 1984. *Inflation Accounting: Reporting of General and Specific Price Changes.* New York: Praeger.

Campbell, T. S. 1982. *Financial Institutions, Markets, and Economic Activity.* New York: McGraw-Hill.

Chamberlain, N. W. 1955. *A General Theory of Economic Process.* New York: Harper.

Debreu, G. 1959. *The Theory of Value.* New York: Wiley.

DeGarmo, E. P. and J. R. Canada. 1973. *Engineering Economy,* 5th ed. New York: Macmillan.

Dohr, J. L. 1924. *Cost Accounting.* New York: Ronald Press.

Edgeworth, F. Y. 1881. *Mathematical Psychics.* London: C. K. Paul & Co.

Ely, R. and R. Hess. 1937. *Outlines of Economics.* New York: Macmillan.

English, J. M., ed. 1968. *Cost-Effectiveness: The Economic Evaluation of Engineered Systems.* New York: Wiley.

Fellner, W. 1960. *Modern Economic Analysis.* New York: McGraw-Hill.

Financial Accounting Standards Board. 1975. *Statement No. 12.* "Accounting for Certain Marketable Securities." Stamford, Conn.: Financial Accounting Standards Board.

Financial Accounting Standards Board. 1976. *Statement No. 13.* "Accounting for Leases." Stamford, Conn.: Financial Accounting Standards Board.

Financial Accounting Standards Board. 1978. *Statement of Financial Accounting Concepts No. 1.* "Objectives of Financial Reporting by Business Enterprises." Stamford, Conn.: Financial Accounting Standards Board.

Financial Accounting Standards Board. 1979. *Statement No. 33.* "Financial Reporting and Changing Prices." Stamford, Conn.: Financial Accounting Standards Board.

Financial Accounting Standards Board. 1980. *Statement of Financial Accounting Concepts No. 2.* "Qualitative Characteristics of Accounting Information." Stamford, Conn.: Financial Accounting Standards Board.

Fisher I. [1892] 1925. *Mathematical Investigations in the Theory of Values and Prices*. New Haven, Conn.: Yale University Press.

Fisher, I. 1930. *The Theory of Interest*. New York: Macmillan.

Fremgen, J. 1966. *Managerial Cost Analysis*. Homewood, Ill.: Irwin.

Friedman, M. 1956. *Studies in the Quantity Theory of Money*. Chicago: University of Chicago Press.

Garner, S. P. 1954. *Evolution of Cost Accounting to 1925*. University, Ala.: University of Alabama Press.

Gilman, S. 1939. *Accounting Concepts for Profit*. New York: Ronald Press.

Goetz, B. 1949. *Management Planning and Control*. New York: McGraw-Hill.

Graham, B., D. Dodd, and S. Cottle. 1962. *Security Analysis: Principles and Technique,* 4th ed. New York: McGraw-Hill.

Hicks, J. R., 1946. *Value and Capital.* 2nd ed. Oxford, Eng.: Clarendon Press.

Horngren, C. 1978. *Introduction to Management Accounting,* 4th ed. Englewood Cliffs, N.J.: Prentice-Hall.

Horngren, C. T. 1982. *Cost Accounting,* 5th ed. Englewood Cliffs, N.J.: Prentice-Hall.

Jevons, W. S. [1871] 1957. *The Theory of Political Economy,* 5th ed. New York: Kelley & Millman.

Johnson, H. L. 1979. *Disclosure of Corporate Social Performance.* New York: Praeger.

Kaplan, R. S. 1983, October. "Measuring Manufacturing Performance: A New Challenge for Managerial Accounting Research." *The Accounting Review.*

Kaplan, R. S. 1984, July. "The Evolution of Management Accounting." *The Accounting Review.*

Keynes, J. M. 1936. *The General Theory of Employment, Interest, and Money.* New York: Harcourt Brace Jovanovich.

Knight, B. W. 1942. *Economic Principles in Practice.* New York: Farrar and Rinehard.

Mansfield, E. 1977. *Economics, Principles, Problems, Decisions,* 2nd ed. New York: W. W. Norton & Company.

Markowitz, H. 1952, March. "Portfolio Selection." *The Journal of Finance.*

Maurice, S. and C. W. Smithson. 1981. *Managerial Economics.* Homewood, Ill.: Irwin.

Modigliani, F. and M. Miller. 1958, June. "The Cost of Capital, Corporation Finance, and the Theory of Investments." *American Economic Review.*

Morse, W. 1981. *Cost Accounting,* 2nd ed. Reading, Mass.: Addison-Wesley.

Most, K. 1977. *Accounting Theory.* Columbus, Ohio: Grid.

National Association of Accountants. 1981. "Definition of Management Accounting." *Statement on Management Accounting No. 1A.* New York: National Association of Accountants.

National Association of Accountants. 1982. "Objectives of Management Accounting." *Statement on Management Accounting No. 1B.* New York: National Association of Accountants.

Neuner, J. and S. Frumer. 1967. *Cost Accounting: Principles and Practice,* 7th ed. Homewood, Ill.: Irwin.

Noyes, C. R. 1948. *Economic Man,* vol. 2. New York: Columbia University Press.

Ouchi, W. 1981. *Theory Z: How American Business Can Meet the Japanese Challenge.* Reading, Mass.: Addison-Wesley.

Polakoff, M. E. 1970. *Financial Institutions and Markets.* Boston: Houghton-Mifflin.

Popper, K. 1959. *The Logic of Scientific Discovery.* New York: Basic Books.

Reich, R. 1983, March. "The Next American Frontier." *The Atlantic Monthly.*

Revsine, L. 1970, July. "On the Correspondence Between Replacement Cost Income and Economic Income." *The Accounting Review.*

Revsine, L. 1973. *Replacement Cost Accounting.* Englewood Cliffs, N.J.: Prentice-Hall.

Rose, P. S. 1983. *Money and Capital Markets.* Plano, Tex.: Business Publications.

Rose, P. S. and D. R. Fraser. 1985. *Financial Institutions,* 2nd ed. Plano, Tex.: Business Publications.

Savage, L. 1954. *The Foundation of Statistics.* New York: Wiley.

Sharpe, W. F. 1963, January. "A Simplified Model for Portfolio Analysis." *Management Science.*

Sharpe, W. F. 1970. *Portfolio Theory and Capital Markets.* New York: McGraw-Hill.

Shillinglaw, G. 1967. *Cost Accounting: Analysis and Control,* rev. ed. Homewood, Ill.: Irwin.

Simon, H. A. 1959, June. "Rational Decision Making in Business Behavioral Science." *American Economic Review.*

Simon, H. A. 1960. *The New Science of Management Decisions.* New York: Harper and Row.

Simon H. A. 1979, September. "Rational Decision Making in Business Organizations." *American Economic Review.*

Solomons, D., ed. 1952. *Studies in Costing.* London: Sweet and Maxwell.

Solomons, D. 1966. "Economic and Accounting Concepts of Cost and Value." In *Modern Accounting Theory,* ed. M. Backer. Englewood Cliffs, N.J.: Prentice-Hall.

Tarascio, V. J. [1906] 1968. *Pareto's Methodological Approach to Economics.* Chapel Hill: University of North Carolina Press.

Thompson, A. A., Jr. 1973. *Economics of the Firm Theory and Practice.* Englewood Cliffs, N.J.: Prentice-Hall.

Tobin, J. 1958, February. "Liquidity Tolerance as Behavior Toward Risk." *Review of Economic Studies.*

Von Neumann, J. and O. Morgenstern. 1953. *Theory of Games and Economic Behavior.* Princeton, N.J.: Princeton University Press.

Walras, L. [1874] 1954. *Elements of Pure Economics.* London: Allen & Unwin.

Wiener, N. 1954. *The Human Use of Beings: Cybernetics and Society,* 2nd ed. Garden City, N.Y.: Doubleday.

Williams, J. 1938. *Theory of Investment Value.* Cambridge, Mass.: Harvard University Press.

Wilson, G. E. 1983, November. "Theory Z: Implications for Management Accountants." *Management Accounting.*

Index